THE CAMERONIANS

THE
CAMERONIANS

A Concise History

TREVOR ROYLE

MAINSTREAM
PUBLISHING

EDINBURGH AND LONDON

First published in Great Britain in 2009 by
MAINSTREAM PUBLISHING COMPANY
(EDINBURGH) LTD
7 Albany Street
Edinburgh EH1 3UG

ISBN 9781845963279

A catalogue record for this book is available
from the British Library

Typeset in Bembo

Printed in Great Britain by
Clays Ltd, St Ives plc

Contents

Preface

Preface

This is the eighth and last in the series of concise histories of the Scottish infantry regiments as they existed up to 1968. At the end of the Second World War Scotland possessed ten line infantry regiments, each with two regular battalions (Royal Scots, Royal Scots Fusiliers, King's Own Scottish Borderers, Cameronians, Black Watch, Highland Light Infantry, Seaforth Highlanders, Queen's Own Cameron Highlanders, Gordon Highlanders and Argyll and Sutherland Highlanders), two battalions of foot guards (Scots Guards) and one cavalry regiment (Royal Scots Greys). Since then the numbers have been reduced by a process of disbandment and amalgamation so that by 2006 there was one infantry regiment with five regular battalions (Royal Regiment of Scotland), one foot guards regiment with one battalion (Scots Guards) and one cavalry regiment (Royal Scots Dragoon Guards). The cutbacks came in the following sequence: in 1947 each infantry regiment had to reduce its strength to a single battalion; in 1959 The Royal Scots Fusiliers amalgamated with The Highland Light Infantry to form The Royal Highland Fusiliers; in 1961 The Seaforth Highlanders joined forces with Queen's Own Cameron Highlanders to form Queen's Own Highlanders; in 1971 The Royal Scots Greys formed The Royal Scots Dragoon Guards with 3rd Carabiniers (Prince of Wales's Dragoon Guards); in 1993 The Scots Guards lost its 2nd battalion which was placed in 'suspended animation'.

During that process of change, which has been a constant recurrence throughout the history of the British Army, the only Scottish disbandment was the loss of The Cameronians (Scottish Rifles) in 1968. Oceans of ink have been used to argue the pros and cons of that decision. Amalgamation with The King's Own Scottish Borderers (KOSB) was one possibility – at the time of the 1959 round of defence cuts some within the regiment thought that it would be amalgamated with The Highland Light Infantry – but when the axe fell in 1967 the decision was taken within the regimental family to disband. Later, many regretted that resolution and even at the time some felt that it had been taken with indecent haste as the final date for oblivion was 1970. However, with the passing of time and with hindsight, it was the correct move. Even if the amalgamation with KOSB had worked, it would only have led to further amalgamations and the dilution of the Cameronian name – in 2006 The Royal Scots and KOSB amalgamated to form The Royal Scots Borderers, 1st Battalion The Royal Regiment of Scotland.

Inevitably those changes created a great deal of sadness in the army community and more widely throughout Scotland, with regret being expressed for the loss of some cherished names and the conversion of the old single battalion regiments into a new formation. However, the history of the British Army shows that the story of its regiments has been one of constant development, with cutbacks, amalgamations and changes of name being part of a process of evolution stretching back over several centuries. In every case the development has not led to a diminution of the army's capabilities but has produced new regiments that are the equal of their predecessors. At least, in the case of The Cameronians (Scottish Rifles), its history is inviolable and its traditions are still intact.

Together with the other books in the series this concise history has been written to mark this latest transformation in Scottish and British military history. This is not a new regimental history of the regiment and its predecessors, but I hope it will be a useful addition to the regiment's historiography. Invariably, as is the case with the other concise regimental histories in the series, it also reflects the history of the British Army and the empire in which it served. I owe a tremendous debt to previous regimental historians, whose books are listed in the bibliography. It goes without saying, I hope, that the history of the regiment could not have been attempted without a thorough reading of these volumes as well as the many personal accounts written by soldiers who served in The Cameronians.

For help with the selection of illustrations I would like to thank the staff at the Cameronians Collection, Low Parks Museum, Hamilton. Grateful thanks are also due to Major Brian Leishman, editor of *The Covenanter* and a regimental trustee, who gave his blessing to the project.

Trevor Royle

ONE

For King and Covenant

In May 1968 The Cameronians (Scottish Rifles) disbanded at Douglas in Lanarkshire at roughly the same spot it had been raised in 1689. It was a sonorous moment; the atmosphere was heavy with history and the sentiments expressed that day reflected the strength of the emotions being experienced by those present: the Rev. Donald MacDonald, a former regimental chaplain, caught the mood when he stated that as the regiment marched out of the Army List into history it was entering a 'proud place' where 'no man can remove your name and no man can snatch a rose from the chaplet of your honour'. It was a moving and prescient comment, but MacDonald's words also ensured that the regiment would survive in the minds of everyone associated with The Cameronians and, beyond it, the greater Scottish regimental family. For 279 years the regiment had been central to the way Scots regarded the army and its loss was a blow to all who had served in its ranks or had family connections with the men who wore Douglas tartan. And yet, the chaplain had the last word. Although The Cameronians are no more and the regiment is unlikely ever to be restored to the Army List, its place in history is unassailable. For many years it was Scotland's only rifle regiment; on parade it marched at 140 paces per minute and its dark rifle-green tunics marked it out as an elite formation. It embraced the history of one regiment, 26th Cameronians, which had its origins in the turbulent period that accompanied the arrival of the House of Orange at the end of the seventeenth century, while its other component part, 90th Perthshire Light Infantry, was raised for service in the war against Revolutionary France. Over the years the regiment has provided the British Army with an impressive number of distinguished soldiers, including three field marshals – viscounts Hill and Wolseley and Sir Evelyn Wood – and during the Second World War no other regiment produced so many senior commanders, including two generals, two lieutenant-generals, five major-generals and 19 brigadiers. Always tough and enduring in battle, The Cameronians reflected the character of its main recruitment area – Glasgow and Lanarkshire – and in later years it took self-conscious pride in the fact that the Germans nicknamed its soldiers *Giftzwerge*, poison dwarfs.

To understand how this proud regiment came into being it is necessary to go back to the death of King Charles II and the succession of his brother King James VII and II in 1685. Initially the new reign got off to a promising start but soon James began a reckless policy of promoting Catholic allies and England became increasingly Catholic in complexion. A papal nuncio was received, new friaries and monasteries were opened in London, a Jesuit school appeared at the Savoy, the army welcomed Catholic chaplains and James began taking soundings amongst Justices of the Peace and deputy lieutenants of the counties about repealing the Test Act. A first Declaration of Indulgence ending laws against Catholics was passed in April 1687 (in Scotland the legislation was passed as Letters of Indulgence) and a second declaration appeared in May the following year. Similar steps were taken in Ireland to unstitch the Protestant ascendancy: Catholics were granted key political and legal appointments and the Irish parliament threatened to pass legislation to reverse the land settlement introduced by Oliver Cromwell in the previous decade. To the watching Irish Protestants the situation seemed ripe for a Catholic takeover.

The flashpoint was provided by the Church. In May 1688 James ordered the second Declaration of Indulgence to be read in all churches; six bishops refused and were put on trial for seditious libel, together with the Archbishop of Canterbury. (They were acquitted amidst great public jubilation at the end of June.) With the king and the Church in direct confrontation, a group of conspirators made contact with William of Orange and invited him to intervene to save parliament and religion, 'if the circumstances stand so with your Highness that you believe that you can get here time enough, in a condition to give assistance this year'. (As the son of Charles II's sister Mary, William had a claim on the throne, as did his wife Mary, who was the daughter of James VII and II.) This was the message James's son-in-law had been waiting for and he immediately began raising an invasion force. William's decision was prompted by one further event – the birth of a son and heir, James Edward Stewart, to his father-in-law and his second wife, Mary of Modena. It was inconceivable that the new prince would not be raised in the Catholic faith.

James attempted to make concessions but it was too late, and he knew it. Following the bishops' acquittal James had been surprised to see his soldiers cheering and was equally astonished when an officer told him not to concern himself. 'Do you call that nothing?' retorted the king. Things were falling apart and when William landed at Torbay on 5 November support began drifting away from the Crown towards the invading saviour. The magnates who had invited William began seizing the key cities, two senior army commanders, the Duke of Grafton and Colonel John Churchill, turned coat, and with no army to defend him James was forced to escape to France. Even that proved difficult. The fishermen taking him uncovered his identity and brought him back, and it was not until the year's end that he was allowed to leave openly through the port of Rochester. The last Stewart king had departed and the dynasty was destined never to return to its three kingdoms.

The end of the Stewarts and the arrival of the Protestant House of Orange finally settled the relationship between the monarch, the parliament and the people. It was enshrined in the Declaration of Rights which was presented to William on 13 February 1689 together with the offer of the Crown; it stated that parliaments must be held regularly, that elections must be free and that its debates must be open and not questioned in any place other than parliament, that only parliament could give consent to statutes, levy taxation and that 'raising and keeping a standing army within the kingdom in time of peace unless it be with consent of parliament is illegal'. The declaration also limited the succession to William's heirs and excluded Catholics. Unlike earlier usurpations there was no bloodshed and the event was known to English history as the Glorious Revolution. Only in Scotland and Ireland was the new order greeted with violence, and as a result the regiment known as The Cameronians came into being. On 14 May 1689 on the banks of Douglas Water in south Lanarkshire, the 19-year-old James Douglas, 14th Earl of Angus and son of the Marquis of Douglas, raised a regiment of infantry to defend the rights of the Convention of Estates and to pledge loyalty to the new joint monarchy of William and Mary of Orange:

> The Estates of the kingdom of Scotland, considering that James, Lord Angus has made an offer to levie a Regiment of 1200 foot, to be commanded by him as Collonel, and to be employed in the service of His Majestie, William, by

the grace of God, King of Great Britain, France and Ireland; and the Estates reposing trust and fidelitie couradge and good conduct of the said James, Lord Angus, have therefore nominated, constituted and appoynted the said James, Lord Angus to be Collonel of the said regiment of foot appoynted by the act of the said Estates of the dait of these presents, to be levied by him as said is consisting of 20 companies, and 60 men in each company, with full power to the said James, Lord Angus to nominate the Lieutenant Collonel and Major of the said regiment, both officers and souldiers, as Collonel and Captain, carefully and diligently, and to keep them in good order and discipline, and to doe and act all things competent and incumbent for any Collonel of foot . . .

The regiment's commanding officer in the rank of lieutenant-colonel was William Cleland, the son of the gamekeeper on the nearby Douglas estates and an experienced soldier who had already seen military service fighting for the cause of the Covenanters, militant Presbyterians, also known as United Societies, or Hillmen, who had opposed the imposition of episcopacy during the reign of King Charles II. Theirs was an austere and unyielding form of religion which demanded discipline and obedience: those who followed it were prepared to fight for their beliefs and in time they were forced to worship in the open, usually in remote upland areas where armed pickets were posted to guard the worshippers and their minister who had been 'outed' from the established Church. As described by Bishop Gilbert Burnet in his justly celebrated memoirs, *History of His Own Time* (1724), the Covenanting ministers seem to have had more in common with the Old Testament prophets:

> They prayed long and with much fervour. They preached twice on Sunday and for most part once on a week day. They catechised all their people at least once a year in their

communions, and they used to visit the families in their parishes oft and to pray to them and exhort them in secret. They had also frequent private meetings, where those that were of a higher dispensation than the rest met, sometimes without the minister and sometimes with him, and used to propose their cases and discourse about them and pray concerning them. And by these means the people, especially in the west, where those practices were frequenter, grew to that readiness, both in discoursing about sacred things and in praying, that it has astonished me to overhear them at these exercises; not but that they had many impertinences among them, yet it was a wonderful thing to me, and perhaps not to be paralleled anywhere, that the generality of the commons should have been able to pray extempore something for a whole hour together.

Many of the men who answered the Earl of Angus's call came from that kind of background and as a result the regiment took its name from one of the foremost Covenanting leaders, Richard Cameron, 'The Lion of the Covenant', whose followers were known as Cameronians. Significantly, one of Angus's first appointments was Alexander Shields as chaplain, and it was also ordained that each company should be provided with an elder 'in order that piety might be promoted and offenders be reproved'. From the outset soldiers were permitted to carry weapons to church and posted armed pickets outside to protect the congregation; this tradition lasted until the final disbandment parade in 1968. In essence the new regiment was as much a congregation as a fighting formation, each man carried a bible and the instructions given to them at their first muster left them all in no doubt that one of their main tasks was the protection of the Presbyterian religion. Each soldier had to enter into the following agreement:

> That they shall be well affected, of approved fidelity and
> of a sober conversation. They declare: that the cause they
> are called to appear for is, the service of the King's Majesty,
> in the defence of the nation; recovery and preservation of
> the Protestant religion; and, in particular, the work of the
> Reformation in Scotland, in opposition to Popery, prelacy
> and arbitrary power in all its branches and steps, until the
> Government of Church and State be brought back to their
> lustre and integrity established in the best and purest terms.

Once mustered, the Cameronian regiment moved north to Perth,
stopping first at Stirling to receive uniforms and weapons – 400
pikes and 400 muskets. Their immediate task was to engage in
internal security duties, guarding the approaches to the Highlands
'to clear the braes of Stirling-shire of lowse [dissolute] and ill-
affected men who might be found in arms'. At the time that the
regiment was raised the Covenanters had largely passed into history
and most of their number had been forced back into the accepted
order. However, not everyone in Scotland was prepared to accept
William as king and the opposition to the new order centred on a
prominent Jacobite (as James's supporters came to be known), John
Graham of Claverhouse, Viscount Dundee, who began gathering
forces in his heartlands north of the Tay. At the same time the Duke
of Gordon seized Edinburgh Castle in James's name. To counter
this threat the Estates appointed Major-General Hugh MacKay of
Scourie to command its forces, which consisted of three regiments
of the Scots Brigade which had been serving in the Low Countries
since 1572 and the Edinburgh Regiment (later The King's Own
Scottish Borderers) which had been raised by the Earl of Leven
two months before the Earl of Angus's regiment came into being.
MacKay offered huge bribes to try to win the support of the clans
but it was an uphill task as Dundee enjoyed the support of clan

chiefs like Cameron of Lochiel and MacDonald of Keppoch, both of whom provided him with armed retainers. Having decided to base himself in Badenoch and Lochaber he slowly built up Jacobite strength and by the end of May had at least 1,700 men under his command. At the end of the month Dundee attacked Ruthven Castle and burned it down in an attempt to lure MacKay into battle, but the commander of the Convention army refused to take the bait. Instead he kept his forces well clear of the Highland area and awaited developments. They were not long in coming. On 22 July 1689 Dundee moved out of Lochaber and advanced towards Blair Castle to confront MacKay's army, which was approaching nearby Dunkeld. At the resulting battle in the Pass of Killiecrankie the Highland forces gained the upper hand, but Dundee's death in the moment of victory meant that the rebellion was over before it had begun – shorn of his inspirational leadership the clansmen started drifting home.

Although Cleland's Cameronians had not been involved in the Battle of Killiecrankie, they were soon in action against the Jacobites. Three weeks later the Jacobite army, now commanded by Brigadier-General Cannon, moved on Dunkeld where Cleland had placed his men in a defensive formation. Knowing that he would be fighting in a built-up area and that he had to avoid unnecessary civilian casualties inside the town, he prepared those defences carefully. Walls were rebuilt and pickets placed at key points, and various houses and the local church were turned into defended positions. To begin with there was some dissent within the ranks that the regiment had been sent to garrison a town with no obvious defences, and these fears were exacerbated by rumours that the officers intended to flee on their horses in the event of things going badly. Cleland was equal to the task. On hearing the tittle-tattle he called the men together and told them: 'Neither I nor any of my officers will, in any extremity, abandon you. Bring out my horse, all our horses, they shall be shot dead.' His words steadied nerves and the men replied that the horses should not be shot and confirmed that all would face 'the last hazard' together.

On 21 August the Jacobite army appeared outside Dunkeld and, as anticipated, its opening gambit was the same fearsome headlong charge into the opposition's lines which had broken MacKay's forces at Killiecrankie. In the first shock the Cameronians' lines wavered but the pickets withdrew to a defensive wall in front of the Marquis of Atholl's house, from which they were able to pour heavy and sustained fire into the Jacobites' lines. Soon some of the surrounding houses were on fire, killing those Jacobite soldiers who had hoped to use them as firing points, and the regimental records reported that the slaughter proved to be 'a terrible initiation for recruits'. During this phase Cleland was shot dead and the battle itself continued for another four hours before the Jacobites began to withdraw in the face of the heavy firing. The regiment's casualties were two officers killed and five wounded and 15 soldiers killed and 30 wounded. The losses in the Jacobite force were estimated at 300 killed, wounded or taken prisoner. In the regimental records the battle was neatly summarised without any self-congratulation: 'That a handful of inexperienced men was wonderfully animated to a steadfast resistance against a multitude of obstinate furies; but they give the glory to God, and praised him, and sung psalms, after they had fitted themselves for a new assault.' Even the defeated side was impressed: in the wake of the fight at Dunkeld a Jacobite song came into common currency ruefully praising the behaviour of the government forces:

> For murders, too, as soldiers true,
> You were advanced well, boys;
> For you fought like devils, your only rivals,
> When you were at Dunkeld, boys.

In fact the Cameronians had broken the back of the Jacobite rebellion and for the rest of the year the regiment was under MacKay's command undertaking internal security duties in the Highland area. Despite the defeat of the Jacobite forces at Killiecrankie and Dunkeld the country was still thick with rumours about an insurrection in the Highlands and the arrival of Catholic supporters from Ireland. One story insisted that the town of Kirkcudbright had been destroyed and when the Cameronians arrived in Stirling the men were told that '10,000 Papists were landed from Ireland with strange instruments of death for despatching Protestants'. For men brought up in the covenanting tradition and possessing an innate hatred of the Catholic and Episcopalian religions this was probably all the encouragement they needed to undertake the regiment's first assignment.

In the spring of 1691, there was a change of direction when the regiment left Scotland to serve in the Army of the League of Augsburg, a coalition formed by England, the United Provinces of the Netherlands, Spain and the German principalities to oppose King Louis XIV of France's expansionist policies in the Netherlands. At the time France was Europe's main power and there were fears that it would use its military superiority to gain hegemony over the continent and cow Spain into submission. Although the fighting in the Netherlands achieved nothing, it introduced the regiment to Britain's traditional campaigning grounds in Europe. In the coming years the Cameronians would come to know Flanders and the Low Countries well, marching, counter-marching and fighting over ground with names that were to become familiar to generations of soldiers and, in time, part of the regiment's many battle honours.

War had been declared on 7 May 1689 – it was known as the War of the League of Augsburg or the Nine Years War – and the first English army to serve in the theatre of war had been a force of 8,000 under the command of John Churchill, who served under Prince George Frederick of Waldeck. It had secured an early victory over the French at Walcourt in August but the replacement of the French commander de Villars by the experienced Marshal François de Luxembourg changed the complexion of the fighting. The following summer he inflicted a crushing defeat on the allies at Fleurus and followed this up by taking Mons and routing Waldeck's army at Leuze. This was followed up in May 1692 by the capture of the fortress at Namur in a brilliant operation masterminded by Marshal de Vauban, the foremost military engineer of the day, who took only seven days to reduce the garrison.

During this period the Cameronian regiment was brigaded with the Scots Guards, Royal Scots and Ramsay's and Hodge's regiments of foot (the latter later became The Bedfordshire Regiment). Also present in the theatre of operations was Hugh MacKay, acting as a brigade commander. During the operations the British regiments did not serve as a separate force but formed brigades made up of three to five regiments or battalions, each one under the independent command of a lieutenant-colonel. The infantry components were equipped with muskets and pikes and each company (apart from grenadiers) consisted of two-thirds muskets and one-third pikes. In battle musketeers fought six ranks deep while the pikemen fought five deep, their task being to guard the line against attack by cavalry. Only gradually was the matchlock musket replaced by the flintlock; another innovation was the introduction of the plug bayonet in the 1690s to replace the pike as the main weapon to counter cavalry.

Following a series of attempts to engage the French army, all unsuccessful, the allies enjoyed a stroke of good fortune at the beginning of August. While on the march at night the allies, under the command of King William III, unexpectedly came across Luxembourg's army at Steenekirk between the Scheldt and the Meuse, some 15 miles to the south-west of Brussels and to the south of the later and better known battlefield of Oudenarde. In the opening stages the French were surprised and their advance guard was quickly overwhelmed but Luxembourg quickly regrouped his forces and was able to draw them up in a new line of battle to meet the expected allied attack. To the British regiments fell the duty of assaulting the French lines (most of their infantrymen were Swiss, then considered to be the best in Europe). On the left flank were the Cameronians, Coutts's (later the Coldstream Guards) and two regiments of the Scots Brigade (MacKay's and Graham's). The right flank was occupied by the cavalry and three other regiments of foot. It was not an easy task as the attackers had to advance over uneven ground and when the actual fighting began it was marked by vicious close-quarter combat which lasted two hours before the French lines began to falter. Seeing that his men were being beaten back, Luxembourg launched the French Guards who were able to stem the breach opened by the attacking British infantrymen. The regimental records of the Cameronians attest to the ferocity of the fighting:

> Never was a more terrible, and at the same time more regular, fire heard; during two hours it seemed to be like continued thunder. The vanguard behaved with such bravery and resolution, that although they received the charge in succession of the enemy's battalions, yet they drove them from a battery of seven pieces of cannon, which, however, they could send away, as the French had cut the traces and carried off the horses. All the regiments distinguished themselves by their courage and perseverance, driving their opponents from hedge to hedge, often firing from muzzle to muzzle through them.

At that crucial stage in the battle, when the allies had gained an advantage which now had to be protected, William lost control.

Instead of reinforcing MacKay's position he followed the advice given to him by the Dutch general, Hendrik Solms, who had replaced Churchill. For reasons that are unclear and make no sense given the tactical situation, Solms decided to withhold the bulk of his army and left MacKay's regiments to face unequal odds. His only comment was chillingly unhelpful: 'Let us see what sport these English bulldogs will make!' The comments of the other protagonists were equally contrary. As the Cameronians and the other seven regiments began a fighting retreat from the French lines and men started falling in multitudes, William burst into tears as he watched the slaughter and exclaimed, 'Oh, my poor English!' (Like many other things during this ill-starred campaign he was wrong on that count, as also taking part in the battle were Royal Scots, the Scots Fusiliers Regiment of Foot (O'Farrel's) and the Edinburgh Regiment.) As for Hugh MacKay of Scourie, a pious man who believed that he was defrauding the Almighty if he was not doing his great work, he returned to the fighting with the fatalistic words, 'The will of the Lord be done.' He was the most senior of the British losses of the 620 officers and men who were killed or wounded at Steenekirk (amongst them was the Earl of Angus, who fell at the head of his regiment); at the time it was a bloody roll-call in a battle which the historian of the British Army, Sir John Fortescue, described as being 'admirably designed and abominably executed'.

After the battle Lieutenant-Colonel Andrew Monro of the Royals was appointed colonel and following the relief of Charleroi the British expeditionary force went into winter quarters. Shortly after the 1693 campaigning season began William, now with 70,000 men under his command, engaged Luxembourg once more at Landen (or Neerwinden) but enjoyed even less success. The French cavalry managed to break into the allied lines, which had been constructed with entrenchments and palisades along a stream called the Landen, a tributary of the River Geet between Brussels and Liège, and having broken the positions in the centre forced William's men to retire from the battlefield. During the first part of the fighting the Cameronian regiment was part of the defensive line on the right flank together with the Scots Fusiliers and the Edinburgh Regiment. Fortunately, Luxembourg chose not to pursue the retreating army, otherwise William would have been forced to sue for peace. Around 20,000 of his army had become casualties, making the Battle of Landen the bloodiest battle fought in Europe for over 200 years. So great was the slaughter that the House of Lords recommended that no British general should ever again serve under the subordinate command of a Dutch soldier, whatever his rank.

However, the fact that William had not been conclusively defeated in the field encouraged him to continue the war despite the fact that it was a drain on the country's exchequer. It also made him more determined than ever to raise the siege of Namur, which had been reinforced by de Vauban and was thought to be impregnable. Around 14,000 French troops under the command of Duke Louis de Boufflers formed the garrison and the strength of their position was confirmed when the opening rounds failed to make any impression on the defences. The defenders were helped by the fact that the outer works to the south were protected by the River Meuse and by the town which lay to the east. During the besieging operations the grenadier company of the Cameronian regiment was one of the formations involved in the attack on the heights at Bouge on 8 July. There were successive attempts throughout the month on 17, 23 and 24 July and it was not until 26 August that the French garrison was finally worn down by the incessant attacks and the need to defend the fortress walls. On 5 September the garrison finally surrendered the castle, marching out with only 5,538 of the original garrison of 15,000. When the campaigning season came to an end in the autumn the Cameronian regiment was allotted the fortress as its winter quarters.

The war was settled by the Treaty of Ryswick on 20 September 1697 and the British regiments were gradually withdrawn. As would happen later, the cessation of hostilities was a signal for parliament to reduce its defence expenditure and shortly after the treaty was signed it was decided 'that all forces raised since 1680 should be disbanded'. This should have been the death knell for the Cameronians – provision was only made for the employment of 10,000 soldiers by the British establishment – but it remained in Flanders on Dutch pay until 1700, when it returned to Scotland to form the garrison at Perth. Although the standing army had been brought under parliamentary control by the Statute of Rights – previously it had been part of the royal household – soldiering was still an unpopular calling in Britain. Partly the anti-militarism arose from memories of Oliver Cromwell and the rule of the major-generals during the Protectorate of the 1650s; partly, too, it came from the poor conditions endured by the private soldier. Pay was low. An infantryman received eight pence per day and a guardsman was only marginally better recompensed at ten pence per day. Deductions for uniform and subsistence lowered this by at least half, with the result that soldiers found it difficult to survive. Quartering was also primitive. There was a handful of barracks in castles and fortresses of considerable antiquity – Edinburgh, Berwick, Portsmouth, Dover, Hull – but most soldiers found themselves being billeted on the local population, a situation disliked by both sides. Matters were marginally better in Scotland, where the need to provide guards in the Highland areas allowed soldiers to live in military control posts.

At the time all soldiers were supposed to be volunteers, and while that principle was observed in the cavalry the infantry often had to resort to the methods of the press gang. It was not unusual for gangs to round up young men or lure them with drink and then sell them into a regiment. To combat this menace the Scottish Privy Council gave each burgh, city and shire a quota of recruits, with fines being imposed by the justices of the peace if these were not kept. During the winters of 1693–94 and 1696–97, whilst serving in Flanders, the Cameronians received drafts of men in this way. As was the case throughout the army at the time, officers' commissions in the regiment were a commodity that could be bought and sold. The average cost of a colonel's rank was anything between £1,000 and £2,000 (today £108,000–£216,000) while an ensign's commission cost £200 (today £21,500). In the cavalry and foot guards the cost of commissions was even higher, but there was never any shortage of takers. In both cases the bulk of the officers were younger sons of the nobility and the landed gentry but in the early days at least, the Cameronian regiment found many of its officers from a clerical background.

A typical example of this class of officer was John Blackader, whose memoirs and diaries provide a vivid picture of life in the regiment in its early days. He was born in 1664, the son of the Rev. John Blackader, the minister of Troqueer in the parish of Dumfries, who had been expelled when King Charles II introduced the Episcopalian form of worship after the Restoration. It was a family of considerable antiquity which had forged several powerful marriage alliances down the years and was connected to the Douglas earls of Angus and the Graham earls of Menteith. One ancestor had served on the Lancastrian side at Bosworth Field in 1485 and another had fought with James IV at Flodden in 1513. Following the Rev. Blackader's expulsion from the Church he turned to the Covenanters and, according to the family history, 'There was scarcely a hill, a moor, or a glen in the southern and western districts of Scotland where he did not hold a conventicle or celebrate a communion.' Turned into a fugitive, he was eventually captured, and arrested and imprisoned in the notorious prison on the Bass Rock in the Firth of Forth which was used to hold those considered to be the most dangerous Covenanters. In 1685 he died from the privations of his imprisonment.

All those experiences had an effect on John, the youngest of the reverend's six children, who had been a constant companion when his father held field conventicles, and the sense of Christian fellowship was a spur to his decision to follow a military career instead of continuing his studies at the University of Edinburgh. It also allowed him to accept the idea that he had joined a God-fearing regiment which understood its antecedents and remained humble in its achievements. Blackader fought at Dunkeld and after the battle he wrote a long letter to his brother describing the action and giving due praise for the outcome:

> Upon their [Jacobites] retreating, our men gave a great shout, and threw their hats in the air, and then all joined in offering up praises to God for so miraculous a victory. I must really say, The Lord's presence was most visible, strengthening us, so that none of the glory belongs to us, but to His own great name; for we clearly saw, it was not by might, our power, nor by conduct (our best officers being killed at first, or disabled) so that we have many things to humble us, and to make us trust and eye Him alone, and not instruments. I pray God help me, not to forget such a great mercy I have met with, not receiving the least hurt, notwithstanding several falling on my right and left hand.

Blackader went with the regiment to Flanders but he was also candid enough to relate that the move did not meet with the wholehearted support of the United Societies who were the heirs to the Covenanting cause. From the outset there had been a good relationship between the two bodies, but the hardliners within the

United Societies were incensed by the regiment's participation in what they considered to be a 'profane and Popish confederacy'. To their way of thinking, instead of opposing the Church of Rome, the Cameronian regiment was now 'going to espouse the cause of the Antichrist, and fight for the Holy See, in league with heretics and Popish idolators'. While Blackader understood that the power of the United Societies was waning as a result of the emergence of the established Church of Scotland in the wake of the advent of William and Mary, like others of his background he was saddened to see the slackening of the links with the old Covenanting cause. Even so, in spite of the parting of the ways, which was inevitable given the changing political circumstances, as late as 1862 the Rev. Alexander Hislop, compiler of *The Book of Scottish Anecdote*, saw in the regiment a manifestation of their founding faith:

> The Cameronians are strictly religious, and ever act upon that principle; making the war a part of their religion, and converting state policy into points of conscience. They fight as they pray, and pray as they fight, making every battle a new exercise of their faith, and believe that in such case as they are, as it were, under the banner of Christ; if they fall in battle, they die in their calling, as martyrs to the good cause, and believe that in thus shedding their blood, they finish the work of their salvation. From such maxims and articles of faith the Cameronians may be slain, never conquered. Great numbers of them have lost their lives, but few or none ever yielded. On the contrary, whenever they believe their duty or religion calls them to it, they are always unanimous and ready, with undaunted spirits, and great veracity of mind, to encounter hardships, attempt great enterprises, despise danger, and bravely run on to death or victory.

Hislop understood that background only too well. In addition to collecting the material for *The Book of Scottish Anecdote* he was the author of *The Two Babylons: Papal Worship revealed to be the Worship of Nimrod and His Wife* (1858), which claimed that Catholicism was a Babylonian mystery cult whose practices were grafted onto Christianity during the reign of the Emperor Constantine. As for Blackader, his career suffered a setback in 1691 – while the Cameronian regiment was in winter quarters at Maastricht he fought a duel with a fellow officer, Lieutenant Robert Murray, and killed him. (The reason for the challenge is unclear, although Blackader admitted to having a 'careless unthinking temper' and his diaries make it clear that strong drink had been taken.) Although Blackader was court-martialled he was given a personal pardon by King William and was promoted captain two years later. On rejoining his regiment he noted in his diary: 'I pray that God would bless and countenance the endeavours I am using here for curbing vice, and furthering reformation: I hope He will, for I think I am upright, and have His glory singly before my eyes. I strive daily to do what good I can, by the example of a holy life.'

TWO

Europe and North America

By 1700 the Cameronian regiment was back in Scotland, but it was only to be a relatively short return to home quarters; within four years it was back in action in Europe fighting in the war known as the War of the Spanish Succession, which broke out in 1701. On 16 September 1701 the exiled James VII and II died in France and one of Louis XIV's first actions was to recognise his son James (also known as the Old Pretender) as King of Great Britain. With that move, and following Louis's claim on the throne of Spain by supporting his grandson Philip of Anjou to succeed the childless King Charles II, another war in Europe was inevitable. On the one side England, Austria and the United Provinces created a military alliance to prevent this blatant French expansionism, while on the other France and Spain combined with the assistance of the German state of Bavaria. Later Portugal and Savoy joined the French alliance.

The scene was set for over a century of armed conflict in Europe and, later, across the globe, as Britain and France vied for superiority while each at the same time fighting to bring about the other's destruction. During that period the British Army was to expand dramatically and to lay the foundations for its modern existence. Between 1700 and 1800 11 new cavalry and 67 new infantry regiments came into being, while the old civilian-controlled Ordnance Board, which provided the logistics and artillery, was transformed to create the Royal Regiment of Artillery and the Corps of Royal Engineers. After 1751 the infantry regiments lost their colonels' names and were numbered 1st to 49th (see below) and at the height of the war in America in the 1770s the strength of the army stood at 80,579. At the same time, its annual cost to the exchequer was over £3 million. While political and strategic considerations made these rapid changes inevitable, one man was responsible for turning Britain into a professional military nation with a well-trained and well-equipped regular army – John Churchill, Duke of Marlborough, the captain-general who was hailed throughout the army as 'Corporal John' or 'the Old Corporal'.

Born the son of a West Country landowner, he was commissioned in the foot guards in 1667 and saw active service in Tangiers and during the fighting against the Dutch. Six years later he transferred to the French army and fought under the command of the great Marshal Turenne, veteran of the earlier Thirty Years War. The experience also brought Churchill into contact with James, Duke of York, Charles II's brother, who raised him to the peerage on becoming king in 1685. In that role Marlborough had virtual command of the forces which put down the uprising led by the Duke of Monmouth, James's half-brother, and he was also responsible for advising James to oppose William's landing three years later. However, the overall commander, the earl of Feversham, advised retreat and the moment was lost. In the aftermath, despite his Jacobite sympathies, Marlborough was given command of the army and sent to Flanders, where he distinguished himself at the Battle of Walcourt, prompting the comment from King William that 'Marlborough in spite of his youth has displayed in this one battle greater military capacity than do most generals after a long series of wars'. However, a fatal tendency to meddle led him to remain in contact with the exiled James and in 1692 he was arrested and placed in the Tower. It took another three years for him to be reconciled to the House of Orange but it was not until 1702 and the succession of Queen Anne that his star began to rise in earnest. In the fighting that followed his appointment as the queen's captain-general Marlborough was to emerge as one of the greatest field commanders produced by the British Army.

He was also that rare beast, a soldier's general. In the words of one of his men, Sergeant John Millner: 'He [Marlborough] secured the affections of his soldiers by his good nature, care for their provisions, and vigilance not to expose them to unnecessary danger, and gained those of his officers by affability; both one and the other followed him to action with such a cheerfulness, resolution and unanimity as were sure presages of success.' Some idea of Marlborough's influence as the nation's commander-in-chief can be seen in the inexorable growth of his army during his period in command. In 1702, at the outset of war, it numbered 31,000 men; by 1706 it had increased to 50,000 and it peaked at 75,000 five years later, before declining to 23,500 in 1713 when Marlborough was no longer in favour.

The Cameronians joined Marlborough's army in the late spring of 1702 and they were destined to serve under him at his great victories of Blenheim, Ramillies, Oudenarde and Malplaquet, battles which underscore the British Army's fighting traditions and which form an important contribution to the regiment's battle honours. When the Cameronian regiment arrived in Flanders it consisted of 44 officers, 104 non-commissioned officers and 736 soldiers. In the first year Marlborough was unable to encourage his Dutch allies to engage the French and the initial period was spent besieging several important fortresses including Venlo, Stevensweert and Liège. At the end of the campaigning season the Cameronians went along with the rest of Marlborough's army into winter quarters in the Netherlands and were not in action again until the spring of 1703. In April that year the regiment was brigaded with 2nd battalion The Royal Regiment (later The Royal Scots), the 10th and 16th Foot (later, respectively, The Lincolnshire Regiment and The Bedfordshire Regiment) and the Scots Fusiliers Regiment of Foot (later The Royal Scots Fusiliers), all under the command of the earl of Derby. The brigade took part in the successful sieges of Bonn and Limburg but the campaign took its toll on all concerned, the regimental records showing that it was 'one of great fatigue to the soldiers, as the marches and counter-marches were incessant, especially during the months of May and June'.

In the following year Marlborough was determined to take the war into Germany and to put pressure on the Bavarian army of the Elector Maximilian Emmanuel which was threatening Vienna while Austrian forces were fighting in north Italy. At first Marlborough hoped to do this by moving his army into the valley of the Moselle but it soon became evident that he would have to go further south and march to the Danube to prevent the French forces under Marshal Tallard from meeting up with the Bavarians. To do that he would have to take the coalition army, numbering 40,000 (soon to be 60,000 as other units joined), complete with artillery, stores and horses over a distance of 250 miles, an operation which required a massive amount of organisation and forethought on the part of Marlborough and his staff. The men of the Cameronians began their long march south on 28 April and like everyone else in Marlborough's army, bar the high command, they were kept in the dark about their final destination. Marching at an average of 12 miles a day with every fourth day a rest day they made good progress and by the end of June they had made contact with the Austrian army under the command of Prince Eugene of Savoy, to the north of Ulm.

The trick now was to take advantage of surprise and to attack the enemy before Tallard's French forces, advancing from the Rhine, joined the Bavarian army which was deployed north of Augsburg along the Danube. On 2 July the first action in the campaign took place 500 feet above the River Danube on the heights of Schellenberg, a commanding position which guarded the approaches to the fortifications at Donauworth. The subsequent battle was marked by close-quarter fighting and it resulted in an inevitably high casualty count. Of the British casualties of 29 officers and 407 soldiers killed and 86 officers and 1,031 soldiers wounded, the Cameronians lost two officers wounded, one sergeant and 18 men killed and three sergeants and 57 soldiers wounded – a high rate considering the regiment only provided four companies for the assault. Watching the battle while it unfolded was John Blackader, now in the rank of captain:

> In the evening I witnessed one of the hottest actions I have seen. It continued from six to eight o'clock. We gained our point, and beat the enemy from their post, and yet we have no reason to boast or think highly of ourselves. The British value themselves too much, and think nothing can stand before them. We have suffered considerably on this occasion, and have no cause to be proud. During the action I was straitened in praying for success and victory to our people, and had not enlargement to seek any thing but that God would get the praise to himself, and work so as the arm of flesh might not rob him of his glory. O that God might reform this army, that good men might have some pleasure in it. When we see what an uncertain thing our life is – now in health, and the next moment in eternity, it

is wonderful we are not more affected by it. I see also that
the smallest accidents give a turn to the greatest actions,
either to prosper or defeat them: that human wisdom,
courage, or any thing else we value ourselves upon, is but
weak and fallible.

That combination of astute military observation and a heightened
religious sensibility is typical of Blackader's narrative style in his
memoirs. Schellenberg has often been overlooked by the historians,
but by inflicting an early defeat on the enemy and securing the
Danube crossing Marlborough paved the way for his great victory
at Blenheim.

A month later, following a game of cat-and-mouse in
which Maximilian Emmanuel refused battle until he received
reinforcements, Tallard's French army eventually joined forces with
the Bavarians. In an attempt to force the issue by provoking the
enemy Marlborough had devastated hundreds of Bavarian villages
but it proved to be a futile exercise. On 10 August Marlborough
received a message from the commander of the Austrian forces,
Prince Eugene of Savoy, informing him that he had made contact
with the opposition, and the two forces met near the villages of
Blindheim (Blenheim) and Oberglau on the confluence of the
rivers Nebel and Danube. Both sides were evenly balanced in
terms of men (some 55,000 apiece) and guns but Tallard was taken
by surprise and was forced to move to an inferior position with
the Danube on his right flank. The plan was that Marlborough's
forces would attack the French on the enemy right while Eugene
would deal with the Bavarians who were drawn up on the French
left. Shortly after midday on 13 August the battle began when the
British left under Lord John Cutts attacked towards Blenheim
while Marlborough moved towards the centre at Oberglau. During
this phase the Cameronians served in Ferguson's Brigade with

2nd Royals and the 15th and 37th Foot (later, respectively, The East Yorkshire Regiment and 1st Royal Hampshire Regiment). At the same time Eugene took on Maximilian's forces in a hard-hitting assault which prevented them from coming to the assistance of the French.

Once across the Nebel, which ran across the battlefield, Marlborough's force lined itself up in a new offensive formation with two lines of infantry protected by two lines of cavalry and by the end of the afternoon, shortly after 5.30, Tallard's centre had been breached and the battle was as good as over. It was a brilliant victory. The French army had been decisively beaten and on the allied right the Bavarians broke under pressure from Eugene and began streaming away from the battlefield. Many of those fleeing were drowned in the Danube and, overall, the losses on the French and Bavarian side spoke only of a terrible defeat – 38,600 killed, wounded or taken prisoner. Amongst them was Tallard, who became a prisoner. In his official report of the battle Marlborough was quick to praise those who had done the fighting – 'the bravery of all our troops on this occasion cannot be expressed, the Generals, as well as the officers and soldiers behaving themselves with the greatest courage and resolution' – but the battle was also a model of coalition warfare in which the two allied commanders, Marlborough and Eugene, had acted in perfect harmony to secure one of the greatest victories over the French since Agincourt, three centuries earlier. Blackader, who was wounded in the throat during the assault, was moved to call Blenheim 'one of the greatest and most complete victories the age can boast of'. The Cameronians' losses were five officers killed and 14 wounded.

After the battle Marlborough's army returned to the Low Countries and with the rest of the British Army the Cameronians enjoyed a well-earned period of rest and recuperation. After the excitements of Blenheim, the following year was something of an anti-climax but between then and 1709 the Cameronians were to be involved in Marlborough's next three victories, which helped to pave the way to a successful conclusion of the conflict at the Treaty of Utrecht in April 1713. These battles and the supporting operations were fought over Flanders, Ghent and Picardy – ground which would be indelibly associated with the history of the British Army in the years to come. The second of Marlborough's great victories was fought on 23 May at Ramillies, to the north of Namur, where the joint French–Bavarian armies were under the command of Marshal Villeroy and Maximilian Emmanuel. Although victory owed something to luck in that Marlborough came across the enemy forces as they were manoeuvring into position, he took advantage of the surprise by immediately attacking the centre, using his coalition forces to assault the enemy lines, while deploying his British regiments, including the Cameronians, to threaten the French left. Overwhelmed, the enemy broke and the combat phase of the battle was over within hours, with the French and Bavarians losing around 15,000 casualties and the coalition one-third of that number. As a result of the victory the Spanish Netherlands were cleared of enemy forces.

The following year saw the French and her allies go on the offensive with the intention of retrieving lost ground in Flanders and preparing the way for a planned invasion of England, using Antwerp as a jumping-off point. Oudenarde, to the south of Ghent, was fought on 11 July 1708. As happened so often in Marlborough's battles, the outcome depended on the infantry's ability to stand firm in the face of close-quarter fire and bayonet charges before the cavalry attacked to roll up the opposition flanks. During the battle the Cameronians formed the first line on the right and some idea of the strains this placed on the infantry can be found in Blackader's account:

Our regiment, properly speaking, was not engaged in the attack; but what was worse, we were obliged to stand in cold blood, exposed to the enemy's shot, by which we had several killed and wounded, for there was heavy firing for about two hours. Throughout the whole course of it I was constantly engaged, sometimes in prayer, sometimes in praise, sometimes for the public, sometimes for myself. We lay all night upon the field of battle, where the bed of honour was both hard and cold; but we passed the night as well as the groans of dying men would allow us; being thankful for our own preservation. I was mercifully supplied with the comforts of life, and wanted nothing good for me. We marched again by day-break, and formed our lines, the enemy making still some appearance; but it was only their rear-guard, which was easily repulsed; so we returned to our camp. I went again through the field of battle, getting a lecture on mortality from the dead. I observe this of the French, that they are the most easily beat and cowed of any people in the world, did we but second Providence in pushing them when the opportunity is put in our hand. Arise, O Lord, and let thine enemies be scattered. Let the fruits of our victories be the advancement of Christ's kingdom on the earth.

When the French finally broke, pursuit proved to be impossible in the failing light with the result that they were given the opportunity of retreating in reasonably good order towards Ghent.

Malplaquet, the fourth of Marlborough's victories, was fought on 11 September 1709 and it proved to be the toughest of the quartet. It was fought to the south of Mons, where the French under de Villars occupied a well-defended position on wooded rising ground. This time the French offered stouter opposition and the infantry was hard pressed to steady the line as the cavalry regrouped. Later, one of Marlborough's officers remembered that the defeat of the French was won at a heavy cost – 'a deluge of blood was spilt to dislodge them'. During the battle the Cameronians lost three officers, including their commander Lieutenant-Colonel Cranston. French casualties were estimated at around 14,000. War weariness gradually crept into the conflict and at the beginning of 1712 Marlborough was replaced by the Duke of Ormond and the resultant peace negotiations at Utrecht brought the fighting to an end. Philip was acknowledged as King of Spain and the Protestant succession was recognised in Britain, but the lasting legacy of the war was the recognition that a balance of power in Europe would take precedence over dynastic rights in the negotiation of future European affairs. That outcome and the emergence of Britain as a major power owed everything to Marlborough's generalship and the abilities and professionalism of the British Army.

The Cameronians left Flanders on 17 August 1713, sailing from Dunkirk to Ireland, which was to be the regiment's home for the next 13 years. Before departing the regiment took its leave of John Blackader, by then a lieutenant-colonel, who resigned from the army in the summer of 1711 and sold his commission for £2,600 (worth £288,000 today). The regiment's deployment in Ireland was interrupted in the autumn of 1715 when it was recalled to help suppress an uprising in support of returning James Edward Stuart, the Old Pretender, to the throne. This had been prompted by the death of Queen Anne in the previous year and the accession of George, Elector of Hanover, who claimed the throne through his maternal grandmother, Elizabeth, a daughter of James VI and I. With resentment growing in Scotland over the Act of Union of 1707, the Old Pretender decided to make a bid for the throne by appealing to Jacobite supporters in Scotland and the north of England but, like all the attempts made in the eighteenth century, he failed to find any widespread backing. In Scotland the military campaign of 1715 was led with great ineptitude by John Erskine, 6th earl of Mar, who is known to history as 'Bobbing John' on account of his many prevarications and his failure to grasp the moment.

According to the regimental records the Cameronians were recalled because of the 'implicit confidence placed by the Government in their tried fidelity' and while the regiment did not take part in the campaign in Scotland which ended in Mar's defeat at Sheriffmuir on 13 November, it was fully involved in suppressing the Jacobite cause in the north of England. Led by the 25-year-old earl of Derwentwater, whom the novelist Tobias Smollett called 'brave, open, generous, hospitable and human', the English Jacobites were doomed from the start. Few supporters heeded their call to rise up against the recently crowned King George I and their meagre forces were easily defeated at Preston on 12 November. During the fighting the Cameronians, commanded by Lieutenant-Colonel Lord Forrester, served as the only infantry regiment in the government army under the command of Major-General Charles Wills, the rest of the force consisting of five regiments of dragoons and one of horse.

As there was a pressing need to attack the Jacobite army before it forced a siege of Preston, Wills ordered the Cameronians to begin the attack with 50 dismounted reinforcements from each of the cavalry regiments. As they were unsupported by artillery they were forced to engage the Jacobites at their barricades and the engagement quickly degenerated into fierce close-quarter fighting. The regimental records take up the story:

> In this attack his Lordship's coolness and judgement were particularly noted. He placed his men in a narrow passage, where they were out of fire, and then entered the street

alone to reconnoitre the rebels' entrenchment; from which, and from the houses, he was exposed to a heavy fire. Having accomplished his object, his Lordship returned, and leading out his men, drew up one division across the street, to keep under by its fire that of the enemy; whilst, with the remainder, the houses were secured; by which a tenable lodgement was effected in the rebels' line of defence. It was in the course of these operations that he received several wounds. An eye-witness of the action states that the men 'upon all occasions behaved with a great deal of bravery and order'.

The following morning the Jacobites were forced to surrender: 75 English and 143 Scottish 'noblemen and gentlemen' and some 1,400 'ordinary Soldiers' laid down their arms and the Jacobite rebellion in the north of England was over. Of the 142 casualties in the government army (killed and wounded), 92 were Cameronians. At the end of the year the regiment returned to Ireland and did not move again until the beginning of 1726, when it moved by sea from Plymouth to bring the Gibraltar garrison up to strength.

At the time the Rock of Gibraltar was under almost constant attack by Spanish forces. However, not only was the garrison of 6,000 well defended but it was also well supplied with provisions brought in from north Africa and the siege proved to be a long-drawn-out and, for the Spanish, unsuccessful, process. Gibraltar had been ceded to Britain in 1713 by the Treaty of Utrecht and although it did not become a Crown Colony until 1830 it was a key naval base which had to be defended against constant Spanish attempts to win it back. As a result the regiment was in frequent action from its arrival until June 1738, when it moved to the Mediterranean island of Minorca. According to the records no action of any great consequence was ever fought but the tour of duty was 'confined to a patient endurance of danger and fatigue, circumstances very trying to the health and temper of the soldiers, and affording little excitement or hope of distinction'. During the deployment the Cameronians suffered 44 casualties, killed, wounded or dead from disease. The deployment in Minorca ended in 1748 when the regiment returned to garrison duty in Ireland.

Three years later the Cameronians underwent the first attempt to standardise the regimental system when King George II issued a Royal Warrant on 1 July to bring some coherence to the army's cavalry and infantry regiments and the Royal Regiment of Artillery. Under its terms a Regular Establishment came into being with the cavalry, the foot guards and the line infantry regiments being numbered in order of precedence to produce two regiments of horse guards, 14 regiments of cavalry, three regiments of foot guards and 49 regiments of foot. As a result the Cameronians became the 26th Regiment of Foot. Colonels continued in name only but as the warrant made clear, numbers, not names, were to be the order of the day:

> No Colonel to put his Arms, Crest, Device or Livery on any part of the Appointments of the Regiment under his command.
>
> No part of the Cloathing or Ornaments of the Regiments to be Allowed after the following Regulations are put into Execution, but by Us [King George II], or our Captain General's Permission.

Under the changes the Cameronians' facings were to be 'pale yellow', the First, or King's, Colour, would be the Union flag, the Second, or Regimental, Colour would be pale yellow with the Union flag in the upper canton with the number of the regiment in the centre within a wreath of roses and thistles on the same stalk. These colours were to remain in being until 1881, when the 26th was amalgamated with the 90th to form The Cameronians (Scottish Rifles) (see Chapter Five).

Apart from a brief return to Scotland between 1754 and 1757 – its first visit in 32 years – Ireland was to be the regiment's home until May 1767, when it moved across the north Atlantic to join the British garrison in North America. Although the French had been expelled from the continent during the earlier Seven Years War (1756–63), running the American colonies was a huge financial burden on the British government. Due to the need to pay for the defence of North America, and to do this through taxation, it was perhaps inevitable that the colonists would take umbrage at rule from distant London. Within eight years of the regiment's arrival that sense of grievance had been fanned into open warfare.

The rebellion was instigated by the imposition of British taxes and restrictions on land settlement and by the American colonists' insistence that these moves were illegal and could only be imposed by their own elected assemblies. London responded by closing ranks, avoided compromise and set about containing the problem with the resident armed forces which had helped to secure the American colonies during the recently ended Seven Years War. Confrontation became unavoidable. At a meeting of a Continental Congress in the autumn of 1774 the leaders of the 'patriots' rejected parliamentary sovereignty and declared that they would not accept British legislation which alienated their rights. Finally, they also called for a boycott of British trade. By the late eighteenth century the 13 colonies had received large numbers of immigrants from Europe and with them the newcomers brought not just a desire for social change but also a need for land. Both aims seemed to be stymied by the far-off London government whose local garrison was not only thought to be repressive but was known to be expensive as well. (One reason for the taxation was the maintenance of the red-coated regiments to protect the colonies.)

As the protests grew and spread to the main towns – New York, Philadelphia, New Jersey – the local governing classes realised that they could be the target of that dissatisfaction and most decided to swim with the tide, becoming the leaders of the rebellion that was about to break.

At the time the 26th was stationed in Lower Canada with the 7th Foot (later The Royal Fusiliers) while the 8th Foot (later King's Liverpool Regiment) was in Upper Canada, but all three were hampered by the fact that each was on a peacetime establishment of under 400 men. Being broken up in a number of small and remote garrisons did not help matters either. This latter point did not go unnoticed by two of the American colonists' leaders, Benedict Arnold, who had previously served in the British Army, and Ethan Allan, who commanded an irregular force known as the Green Mountain Boys. Both had noted the weak state of the British garrison and in May 1775 Arnold suggested that an initial thrust should be made towards a position at Ticonderoga between Lake Champlain and Lake George which protected the main supply route between Canada and the Upper Hudson Valley. The fort was garrisoned by 60 men of the 26th under the command of Captain Delaplace and the regimental records underscore the fact that its remoteness, combined with American cunning, were to be its undoing:

> Allan, who had often been at Ticonderoga, had remarked a great want of discipline in the garrison, and the negligence of its commander was such that the gates were never shut; disposing his small force in the woods, he went to Captain Delaplace, with whom he was well acquainted, and prevailed on him to lend him twenty men, for the pretended purpose of assisting to transport some goods across the lake. Having contrived to make these men drunk, at nightfall, drawing

his own people from their ambuscade, he advanced to the fort, of which he immediately became master. As there was not one person awake, though there was a sentry at the gate, they were all taken prisoners owing to the shameful negligence of the officer, and the drunkenness of the men.

Bad though that was, worse followed as the loss of the fort gave the colonists much-needed artillery, including a number of mortars and over 100 cannon. Two days later a second British fort at Crown Point also fell into American hands and the captured British soldiers were taken into custody and marched through Vermont to Hartford in Connecticut. There was some measure of revenge in September when Allan's Green Mountain Boys were surprised near Montreal by a small British force under the command of Major Campbell of the 26th. In the subsequent action Allan and 16 others were killed while over 40 men were taken prisoner. Elsewhere, the garrison at St John's was formed by 550 men of the 7th and the 26th who came under the command of Major Charles Preston of the 26th and it was imperative that it should not fall to the Americans who were now massing in two columns, one commanded by Arnold, the other by Richard Montgomery, an Irishman and a former British Army officer. Their intended target was the capture of Quebec and its capture was made more likely when Preston's small garrison at St John's was forced to surrender on 13 November. Montgomery was then able to advance quickly on Montreal which was quickly evacuated with the garrison, including 150 men of the 26th, moving to Quebec. During the operation the regiment almost lost its colours when the fleeing detachment fell into rebel hands. Having removed the colours from their staves they were wrapped around the body of a Cameronian officer, but it was only a temporary respite. When it became clear that escape was impossible the colours were wrapped round cannon balls and hurriedly dropped into the

St Lawrence River to prevent them falling into enemy hands, the ultimate disgrace for any military formation.

In the aftermath of these late winter moves Quebec was besieged by Arnold, but without siege artillery he faced a hopeless task. With the coming of spring three British warships and five transports arrived in the Gulf of St Lawrence bringing reinforcements including fresh drafts of men from Scotland for the 26th. In the autumn the reconstituted regiment was able to leave Canada in the company of the 7th and moved to New York, where it formed part of a brigade-sized force with the 52nd (later 2nd Oxfordshire and Buckinghamshire Light Infantry) and a number of German and friendly American troops, all under the command of Lieutenant-General Sir Henry Clinton. They were in action almost immediately when Clinton attacked the American garrisons at Fort Montgomery and Fort Clinton near Verplanck Point, a precipitous position above the Hudson. Both forts were surprised and captured, with the 26th using the bayonet in its attack. However, as the regimental records make clear, 'this enterprise, which was so highly honourable to the troops employed, was not productive of any advantage'.

By then the British strategy was beginning to unravel. Earlier in the summer of 1777 General Sir William Howe had divided his forces, leaving half of them in New York under Clinton's command and moving the rest south to Chesapeake Bay to threaten Philadelphia, which fell in September following a successful engagement with Washington's forces on the River Brandywine. It was to be Howe's only success that year but, perversely, it led to disaster for the British forces in America. While Howe was taking Philadelphia another force under General Sir John Burgoyne had pressed south from Canada and he desperately needed support. At first things had gone well for Burgoyne. He moved down the Hudson Valley but the going was hard and his soldiers began to falter in the autumn rains and difficult terrain. As each day passed supplies began to run low, morale slumped in the face of constant ambushes and, finding himself heavily outnumbered by the opposition, Burgoyne was forced to surrender to the American commander Horatio Gates at Saratoga on 17 October. He was just 50 miles short of Albany where a British force under Clinton was waiting to join up with him. For the British this was a disaster. An army had fallen into American hands and to make matters worse the defeat at Saratoga encouraged the French to lend assistance to the American cause.

Philadelphia was evacuated in the summer of 1778 and while it is known that the 26th remained under Clinton's command – by then he had succeeded Howe – the regimental records for this period are sparse. With the war moving into the southern theatre of the Carolinas the 26th was withdrawn from North America at the end of 1779 and went into quarters at Tamworth in Staffordshire to recruit. At the time the regiment's strength was only 172 rank and file. The return to England was followed by a move to Shrewsbury and by January 1782 the 26th's numbers had doubled. A year later it returned to Scotland to be based at Musselburgh outside Edinburgh and in October that year it moved over to Ireland for a deployment which lasted three years. During that period, on 16 February 1786, it was notified by the Adjutant-General in Dublin that the title 'Cameronian' would be restored:

> His Grace, the Lord Lieutenant [of Ireland], has received a letter from Sir George Yonge, Secretary at War, acquainting his Grace that his Majesty has been most graciously pleased, at the request of Major-General Sir William Erskine, to grant his Royal permission that the 26th Regiment may in future assume the title of the 26th or Cameronian Regiment of Foot.

At the time Erskine was the regiment's colonel and had clearly instigated the change of title. A year later the regiment assembled at Cork to board the transports *Lord Shelburne* and *General Eliott* for the transatlantic crossing which took the 26th back to Canada. The records show that the regiment consisted of 21 officers, 16 sergeants, ten drummers and 340 rank and file. On arrival it was based on the north shore of the St Lawrence at Beauport, Charlesbourg and other villages in the vicinity of Quebec. In the following year, 1788, it moved to Montreal and for the next 12 years it was involved mainly on internal garrison duties and guarding the border with the United States. By then Britain was at war again with France. Following the upheavals of 1789, which had seen the usurpation and execution of the French royal family, the revolutionaries plunged Europe into 23 years of warfare which would eventually see the rise of a new emperor, Napoleon Bonaparte, and ultimately his defeat at Waterloo. To meet that crisis the 26th was moved to Halifax, Nova Scotia, and in September 1800 embarked for England on board three transports. During the voyage, one of the ships was apprehended in the English Channel by a French privateer and under the conventions of the day the men were released on condition that they would not provide further military service until an exchange had been arranged. As surety two officers of the 26th, Lieutenant Edward Shearman and Ensign Adam Campbell, remained in French hands as hostages and were not released until later in the year, when they returned to the regiment after travelling through Portugal.

THREE

The War against Napoleon

When Britain embarked on its war with revolutionary France it was ill-equipped to do so. Following the Seven Years War and the subsequent loss of the American colonies the navy had been reduced in size and the army was limited to 50,000 effectives. Most importantly, in the initial stages of the fighting Britain lacked the military means to enforce its will on the continent. Years of cutbacks and inefficiency had left it with a majority of soldiers who, according to the historian Major-General John Strawson, were mostly 'down-and-outs, jailbirds and delinquents, who had enlisted for drink as a last resort and were subject to rigid drilling, harsh discipline and unimaginative training'. If the country had possessed an expeditionary force, or, at the very least, a large enough army capable of immediate deployment in France, a pre-emptive strike on Paris could have discommoded the opposition, but such a force was not available to the prime minister, William Pitt the Younger. Instead he had to make do with what he had and that meant deploying some 5,000 men under the Duke of York to Flanders where they were joined by 13,000 of the king's

Hanoverians and some 8,000 Hessian mercenaries. Most of the men were untrained, ill-equipped and unsure what they were meant to be doing, and their efforts were only redeemed by their courage and forbearance and by the willingness of their officers to learn lessons as the campaign progressed. Even so, the deployment was not a credit to British arms. An attempt to take Dunkirk ended in disaster and everywhere the forces of Revolutionary France were in the ascendant. At the end of that first campaign the adjutant-general wrote to a colleague complaining that Britain possessed 'the most undisciplined, the most ignorant, the worst provided army that ever took the field'. It would be at least a decade before well-trained land forces could be deployed in any strength against the numerically superior French army.

At the outset of the fighting Pitt thought that Britain's military contribution would be secondary and that sea power would be the key to victory. As a result of this mistaken diagnosis much of the early effort was spent waging a trade war mainly in the West Indies, which proved to be a death trap for the regiments serving there during the 1790s. During that period the army lost 80,000 men, half of whom succumbed to disease, mainly yellow fever, while the other half was rendered ineffective. The other effect was to hinder recruiting: young men were unlikely to volunteer their services if it meant that they would most likely be killed in the tropics while being prevented from taking their chances closer to home on the battlefields of Flanders. At the same time France became invincible on the continent. Following the British retreat from Dunkirk Prussia made peace with France and in 1797 the Austrians also sued for peace, a move which gave France possession of Belgium and the Rhine frontier. While these events were unfolding Britain embarked belatedly on a programme of military reforms. In 1794 the Duke of York became commander-in-chief and instituted a number of important changes: experienced officers received promotion, an infantry training manual was introduced and the first steps were taken to create a Corps of Riflemen, light infantry soldiers equipped with muzzle-loading rifles similar to the *Jäger* troops used by the Germans and Austrians who operated as scouts and skirmishers in forward positions.

Even so, Britain was in a parlous position. By 1797 its only European ally was Portugal and a new threat had emerged in France, where an artillery officer called Napoleon Bonaparte had become the country's leading military commander and a key member of the Directorate, the country's ruling body. His idea was to take advantage of Britain's isolated position and its stretched naval resources by taking the war to the colonial holdings in India. As a first step for that ambitious plan French naval and land forces were despatched to Egypt in 1798. Although these were initially successful in taking control of the country, which was under the suzerainty of the Ottoman Empire, retribution was not long in coming. The French move was followed by the despatch of a British fleet under the command of Rear-Admiral Horatio Nelson, which promptly destroyed the French fleet at Aboukir Bay (the Battle of the Nile), thereby marooning Napoleon's land forces in Egypt. The victory encouraged Austria and Russia to declare war on France to create the Second Coalition.

26TH CAMERONIAN REGIMENT OF FOOT

Following its return from Canada the 26th had been based at Portsmouth, where it had rebuilt its strength. At the beginning of 1801 it numbered 24 officers, 31 sergeants, 14 drummers and 462 rank and file, all under the command of Lieutenant-Colonel Lord Elphinstone. On 28 May they embarked on the troopship *Madras*, which took the regiment to Egypt to support the expeditionary force which had landed there two months earlier under the command of General Sir Ralph Abercromby.

Although the 26th was not involved in the first phase of the operations which saw the defeat of the French forces at Aboukir Bay, it provided reinforcement during the summer and landed in Egypt in time to take part in the operations to capture Alexandria, which duly fell on 3 September. To recognise their courage all the regiments involved in the expedition (including the 26th) were granted the right to bear on their colours the figure of the Sphinx superscripted with the word 'Egypt'. Some of the gloss was taken off the victory when large numbers of the regiment succumbed to ophthalmia (conjunctivitis or severe inflammation of the eye), with the result that soldiers had to proceed in file led by the man least affected. On 23 October the 26th embarked on three troopships at Alexandria and landed at Falmouth in February the following year. As a result of the victory the French were evicted from Egypt and there followed a temporary and ultimately unsatisfactory truce through the Peace of Amiens, which was negotiated in the winter of 1802–03.

This arrangement was by no means perfect but at least it gave Britain a much-needed breathing space. It also provided Napoleon with the opportunity to rethink his strategy by courting Spain in order to gain possession of Louisiana in North America and Elba and Parma in the Mediterranean. He also laid claim to Malta, which had been captured by Britain in 1800 and was a vital strategic base for controlling the Mediterranean. Having cowed most of Europe Napoleon's ultimate aim was to invade Britain with an army 200,000-strong which included the majority of his most experienced field commanders. But in October 1805 the enterprise was foiled by Nelson's famous victory at Trafalgar, where the French and Spanish fleets were destroyed. Even so, it was a moment of supreme danger. Acting on the belief that the Treaty of Amiens had settled the nation's security, the government under Prime Minister Henry Addington had introduced savage cuts in the armed forces in order to pay for the war. The army had been halved, with its strength set at 95,000 together with a garrison of 15,000 in Ireland and a part-time militia of 50,000. There had to be a complete rethink of military policy when Britain declared war on Napoleonic France in May 1803. As had been forecast, the truce was shortlived and once more the army had to expand to meet the threat of invasion and the longer-term aim of defeating Napoleon's Grande Armée, which numbered 200,000 soldiers in seven army corps, commanded by soldiers of the calibre of Bernadotte, Marmont, Davout, Soult, Lannes, Ney and Augereau.

The 26th was based in Plymouth for the rest of the year and immediately set about attracting new recruits: 80 men were found from the Royal Irish Fencibles but a recruiting party sent to Scotland only succeeded in rounding up 20 volunteers. In an attempt to redress the problem the regiment returned to Scotland at the end of 1802, being based variously in Edinburgh, Stirling and Fort George. However it proved to be barren territory and as a result a new recruiting party travelled to Ireland and returned with some 20 recruits, the majority from Kilkenny. At the time the population of Scotland was around 1.8 million and the martial spirit of earlier years seemed to have evaporated. As a result of the difficulties in finding sufficient numbers of soldiers and the resumption of war with France the government was forced to radically rethink its recruitment policies. All recruiting was halted and instead men were found from the militia and chosen by ballot, a system which permitted the use of substitutes in return for an agreed fee. For example, one Cameronian recruit, a bookbinder, received £100 (£7,220 today) from a tradesman in Falkirk who clearly was not anxious to serve king and country. As the adult male population was obliged to serve in the militia if balloted, the system worked and in 1806 alone 28,000 men were recruited in this way. For the 26th the results were immediate: by the end of

1803 the regiment was 1,000-strong and a 2nd battalion had been formed. Based at Linlithgow and Bo'ness it largely provided drafts for the 1st battalion. Early in December 1/26th marched to Port Patrick by way of Glasgow, Kilmarnock and Ayr prior to a move to Ireland. It was followed almost immediately by 2/26th and the two battalions moved south to the Curragh of Kildare.

Ireland was to be home to both battalions until the end of 1805, when 1/26th formed part of a British expeditionary force sent to Hanover to support a new Third Coalition with Austria and Russia. All told, the battalion consisted of 32 officers, 54 sergeants, 22 drummers and 882 rank and file plus 97 women and 41 children. Two of the three transports ran into difficulties before they reached the German coast. The *Maria* ran aground on a shoal off Texel and quickly foundered with the loss of all hands except for two officers and a small number of men who managed to reach dry land to raise the alarm. Worse followed when the *Aurora* also ran aground, this time on the Goodwin Sands, and was wrecked with the loss of the headquarters company under the command of Major Christopher Davidson. In this double catastrophe 1/26th lost 14 officers and 474 rank and file. Only four companies managed to reach their destination but they remained in Germany for a mere six weeks as Napoleon's great victory at Austerlitz removed the need for British forces. On its return in February 1806 the battalion moved into quarters in Deal and it did not return to Ireland until the summer of 1807. At the same time 2/26th returned to Scotland to begin recruiting in the Glasgow area.

In 1807 the 1st battalion returned to Ireland to begin recruiting, but the returns proved to be very poor and by the beginning of the following year it numbered only 514 rank and file. Drafts continued to come from the 2nd battalion – Dumfries provided 80 men – but recruiting in Ireland was made more difficult by the introduction of a policy which denied choice to militiamen wishing to transfer to the line infantry. It was not until the summer of 1808 that the 1st battalion was brought up to strength again, thanks mainly to the efforts of the 2nd battalion, which provided two large drafts of 265 and 212 recruits. By the time the 1st battalion received orders to join the army of Lieutenant-General Sir David Baird, which was being raised for service in Portugal and Spain, it numbered 49 officers, 53 sergeants, 22 drummers and 866 rank and file under the command of Lieutenant-Colonel William Maxwell. On arrival at Corunna the battalion formed a brigade with 3/1st Foot (The Royal Scots) and the 81st Foot (later 2nd Loyal Regiment).

The reason for their presence in northern Spain had come about as a result of Napoleon's plans for the total blockade of Britain, a plan known as the Continental System, which would only work if the Iberian peninsula were cut off. After the renewal of hostilities in 1803 France quickly defeated Prussia, Austria and Russia, and to complete the domination of Europe Napoleon turned his attention to Spain and Portugal. The first was subjugated by forcing the Spanish King Charles IV to abdicate and imposing military rule in the country under Napoleon's brother Joseph. Portugal, England's oldest ally, was then invaded from Spain by an army commanded by Marshal Junot. Both were daring plans but both were foiled by the refusal of the people of Spain and Portugal to accept French domination and by the British decision to assist them in resisting the invasion by sending forces under the command of Lieutenant-General Sir Arthur Wellesley, a battle-hardened veteran of the wars in India. The first part of the campaign ended in farce. Following a stunning British victory at Vimiero on 21 August 1808 the French army was allowed to retreat back to France in ships provided by the Royal Navy, an agreement which allowed Napoleon to assume command of military operations in the peninsula. At the same time a new British force under the command of Major-General Sir John Moore marched from Lisbon into northern Spain through

Salamanca towards Valladolid, his aim being to link up with friendly Spanish forces.

Almost immediately things started to go wrong. Not only were the British forces ill-prepared to make a long incursion into Spain but the French had not been idle. Napoleon had assembled a huge army of 250,000 men and in December he moved rapidly against Moore's smaller force of 20,000, taking with him 80,000 crack troops of the 'Old Guard' and two of his best marshals, Soult and Ney. The French move took them towards the north-west and by the time that Moore reached Salamanca he realised that he was badly outnumbered – reinforcements had been delayed and did not disembark until the beginning of November – and that Napoleon was now within striking distance. Initially Moore hoped to attack a smaller French force under Soult at Burgos but the move only stung Napoleon into a greater determination to crush the British. On Christmas Eve Moore received further intelligence of Napoleon's intentions: the French army had crossed the Guadarrama mountains and were less than 20 miles away. If he continued he would risk annihilation and so the order was given to fall back on Corunna, where the navy had been ordered to evacuate them.

So began an epic retreat across the snow-covered mountains. It was an operation which demonstrated great courage and determination, but it was also marred by scenes of drunken rampaging as the British soldiers looted the areas through which they passed. By the year's end Moore's army had passed through the relative safety of Astorga and when Napoleon arrived in the same place on New Year's Day he realised that there would be no pitched battle as his enemy had escaped. Instead of continuing the pursuit he left the rest of the operation in the hands of Ney and Soult and, having been warned of a plot against him, returned to Paris. Two weeks later Moore reached Corunna to find that the fleet had been delayed. There was now no option but to engage the French; during the hard-fought battle Moore was mortally wounded and was carried to a rear area. Of the 30,000 British soldiers who marched into Corunna and engaged the French in battle some 24,000 were eventually evacuated. Although the 26th had escaped reasonably lightly during the fighting the voyage back to Plymouth was a desperate business for all concerned, as the regimental records make clear:

> Most of the women, who had been allowed to follow their husbands in the proportion of six to each hundred men, succeeded in effecting their escape, and many had accompanied them through the whole campaign, having suffered almost incredible hardships. The condition of all ranks, when on board, was wretched, as the officers were without baggage, and the men's kits were reduced nearly to nothing; their health became impaired from want of cleanliness, which, without the necessary change of clothes, and the crowded state of the vessels, could not be attained. Disease broke out amongst them on the passage, and in their removal from Plymouth and Portsmouth to other parts higher up the Channel. Numbers were landed and sent into the hospital, of whom many never recovered; whilst the remainder were gradually collected at the quarters assigned for the several corps.

When 1/26th Cameronians re-assembled at Horsham at the end of February 1809 there were only 403 men fit for duty and it took a draft of over 200 militiamen, many from Lanarkshire, to bring the battalion back up to strength. During the summer it was brigaded with 5th Foot (later Royal Northumberland Fusiliers), 23rd Foot (later Royal Welch Fusiliers) and 32nd Foot (later 1st Duke of Cornwall's Light Infantry) for an operation to attack French positions at Walcheren in Flanders. Although the numerically superior British force captured Flushing the French moved their fleet to Antwerp, leaving the British forces isolated on Walcheren Island. They were not withdrawn until the beginning of December, by which time over 4,000 soldiers of the original force of 39,000 had succumbed to fever. The 26th's casualties amounted to 224, a hard blow, especially as the 120 left behind at Corunna were 'never afterwards heard of'. In April 1810 the battalion served on internal security duties in London during the riots occasioned by the arrest of the radical Member of Parliament Sir Francis Burdett, and this was followed by a move to Jersey.

In the summer of 1811 1/26th Cameronians was warned for foreign service and on 23 June left for Portugal on board three transports to join the British 1st Division under the command of Lieutenant-General Sir Brent Spencer. On departure the battalion numbered 33 officers, 34 sergeants, 21 drummers and 618 rank and file, the increase in numbers having been assisted by the arrival of men from the Stirlingshire Militia. The Peninsula Army was under the command of Arthur Wellesley, now ennobled as Viscount Wellington; his earlier victories at Busaco and the Lines of Torres Vedras had enabled Portugal to be liberated the previous year and as a result the focus of the war turned to Spain.

This proved to be a frustrating time for the battalion. There was little contact with the French – Wellington had famously promised 'as this is the last army England has, we must take care of it' – and the battalion missed the operations to take Ciudad Rodrigo and Badajoz due to sickness. This was caused by local conditions and the extreme heat, but in the case of 1/26th Cameronians it was also a hangover from Walcheren. Following an inspection by Lieutenant-General Sir Thomas Graham at the beginning of 1812 1/26th Cameronians was ordered to return to Portugal before moving south to Gibraltar to exchange places with the 82nd Foot (later 2nd South Lancashire Regiment). It proved to be a happy posting. Stringent measures were introduced to improve hygiene, quarantine was established and as a result the scourge abated. By 1814 the battalion had recovered, leaving the records to note that Gibraltar had been 'one of the best stations' for the regiment. During this period the 2nd battalion had remained in Scotland and it was disbanded on 24 October 1814 as a result of the defeat of Napoleon.

90TH PERTHSHIRE VOLUNTEERS

Thomas Graham of Balgowan, the inspector of the stricken 1/26th Cameronians, was one of the most extraordinary Scots of his generation. Born in 1748, he counted the great Marquis of Montrose amongst his kinsmen and was educated at Oxford and in Europe, where he became fluent in French and German and took up a lifelong interest in agricultural improvement. Marriage to the Honourable Mary Cathcart gave him a wife who was one of the great beauties of her day – she was painted four times by Thomas Gainsborough – but her early death from consumption in France in 1792 prompted Graham to join the army as a volunteer private soldier. The episode is recounted in Sir Walter Scott's poem 'The Vision of Don Roderick':

> Nor be his praise o'erpast who strove to hide
> Beneath the warrior's vest affection's wound;
> Whose wish Heaven for his country's weal denied;
> Danger and fate he sought, but glory found.
> From clime to clime, where'er war's trumpets sound
> The wanderer went; yet Caledonia! still
> Thine was his thought in march and tented ground:
> He dreamed 'mid Alpine cliffs of Athole's hill,
> And heard in Ebro's roar his Lynedoch's lovely rill.

One reason for his decision to don uniform was patriotism, as Graham abhorred what was happening in Revolutionary France, considering Napoleon to be a threat to world peace. Another was the disrespectful treatment meted out to his wife's body by a drunken French mob as he brought it back from France to be buried in the churchyard at Methven in Perthshire. The other result of this incident was his decision to apply for permission to found an infantry regiment and after some prevarication – King George III was concerned about Graham's lack of military experience – the new formation came into being on 10 February 1794 as 90th Perthshire Volunteers. (It was the third regiment to hold that number, previous regiments having served 1759–63 and 1779–83.) The uniform consisted of a red 'wing jacket' faced with buff, over a red waistcoat; the officers wore buff tights, the men light grey cloth pantaloons, hence the corps was dubbed the 'Perthshire Grey-Breeks'. The headwear was a leather helmet of dragoon pattern, with black bearskin crest and brass-bound peak, and a tall green hackle feather at the side. When the regiment was mustered in May it consisted of seven officers and 746 rank and file. Of these 95 were Scottish Highlanders, 430 Scottish Lowlanders, 165 English and 56 Irish.

This encouraged the raising of a 2nd battalion which was placed under the command of Graham's cousin, Lieutenant-Colonel Alexander Hope. Once raised, the new battalion was transferred to the Royal Marines to help meet the need for 'sea soldiers'. Although Marines had no part to play in the operation of ships, they had a vital role in battle – from providing firepower from the poop, quarterdeck and forecastle to repelling boarders. They also produced the manpower for boarding parties and were used in landing parties, where they fulfilled the same function as infantry. Following the successful use of Marines during the amphibious operations at Belleisle during the Seven Years War, when two battalions joined nine infantry battalions to capture the French possession, the numbers of Marines was increased to 19,000. Marines also took part in many of the operations during the American War of Independence, fighting both ashore and on the warships operated by the Royal Navy.

Having raised his regiment Graham was anxious for it to take up its place in the British Army and on 27 June 1794 it moved south by sea to Hampshire where it remained until the following summer. Its first taste of active service came in amphibious operations to support French Royalists on the island of L'Isle Dieu off the coast of Brittany. Although the battalion succeeded in landing, the collapse of the French royalists meant that the men had to be re-embarked almost immediately and returned to Poole in Dorset. From there the 90th moved to Gibraltar, where it began training as a light infantry regiment whose tactics were similar to those of the new Corps of Riflemen. From there it joined a force including the 42nd Highlanders (later 1st Black Watch) which took part in the operations to seize the island of Minorca in November 1798. During these operations the regiment consisted of 23 officers, 51 sergeants, 22 drummers and 748 privates. Following the successful landings the regiment received another piece of good news when a letter arrived from London announcing that a lottery ticket purchased in the 90th's name had drawn a prize worth £20,000 and that this would be shared equally amongst the officers and men. Taking Minorca was a prelude to the next stage of a Mediterranean policy which would take a British field army under Ralph Abercromby to oust French forces from Egypt and to relieve the threat which they posed to Britain's holdings in India (see above).

While the preparations were being made, command of the regiment passed to Lieutenant-Colonel Rowland Hill, the future field marshal, and he quickly divined that the operation would be a hazardous undertaking. Not only were the French already in position at Alexandria, but they had more artillery, possessed cavalry and were in a good position to oppose the amphibious landings. However, thanks to strict training in advance of the landings the British force came safely ashore at Aboukir Bay on 8 March 1799 and quickly formed a beach-head, forcing the French to withdraw. The respite was only temporary, however, and the 90th was in action again four days later to repel the inevitable counter-attack at Mandora where French cavalry attacked the 90th and the 92nd Highlanders (later 2nd Gordon Highlanders) on the morning of 13 March. The action was described by Major-General Sir David Stewart of Garth in his history of the Highland regiments:

> When the army had cleared the date trees the enemy quitted the heights, and with great boldness moved down on the 92nd, which by this time had formed in line. The French opened a heavy fire of cannon and musketry, which the 92nd quickly returned, firmly resisting the repeated attacks of the French line (supported as it was by a powerful artillery) and singly maintaining their ground till the line came up. At the same time the French cavalry, with the greatest impetuosity, charged down a declivity on the 90th regiment. This corps, standing with the coolest intrepidity, allowed them to approach within fifty yards, when, by a well-directed fire, they so completely broke the charge, that only a few reached the regiment, and most of them were instantly bayoneted; the rest fled off to their left, and retreated in the greatest confusion. The 90th regiment being dressed in helmets, as a corps of light infantry, were mistaken for dismounted cavalry, and the enemy, believing them out of their element, attacked with more boldness as they expected less resistance.

The main battle took place on 21 March at Canopus between Aboukir and Alexandria and it was a ferocious business with the French losing at least 4,000 casualties and the British half that number, one of which was Abercromby. The losses in the 90th were 22 rank and file killed and eight officers and 214 rank and file wounded. Under the operational direction of Major-General John Moore the defending British forces showed great coolness under fire and a month later Alexandria was in their hands. In a letter to Thomas Graham, dated 4 April, Rowland Hill provides confirmation that the 90th had engaged in battle as a light infantry regiment, using bugle calls to give orders:

> The enemy was on commanding ground, and we kept up a very heavy fire of grape and musketry. We advanced and drove the French from the first position. I then, with the bugle-horn, halted the regiment and ceased firing, and, correcting our line, advanced with the greatest regularity to the second hill, where we were opposed with a very heavy fire; we had nearly gained the height, when I was wounded and fell from my horse, and carried out of the field. The enemy continued to retreat till he arrived at his present position. I am convinced it will give you great pleasure that your regiment behaved well . . .

To recognise their courage all the regiments involved in the expedition were granted the right to bear on their colours the figure of the Sphinx superscripted with the word 'Egypt'. As a result of the victory Egypt was saved and there followed a temporary and ultimately unsatisfactory truce with the Peace of Amiens, which was negotiated in the winter of 1802–03.

At the end of the year the 90th moved to Malta, where Hill instituted a number of improvements for the men's well-being. A sergeants' mess was created, as was a regimental school under the tutelage of Lance-Sergeant Anderson. At the beginning of 1802 the regiment returned to England before moving to Fort George in preparation for a deployment in Ireland. The following year Hill left the regiment, having been promoted brigadier-general, and whilst in Ireland the 90th continued training as a light infantry regiment. A letter from Graham dated 29 January 1804 underlined the importance of this point and provides an insight into the differences between line infantry regiments and the new light infantry regiments:

> The leading principle that should govern the conduct of all officers is to prevent their men being exposed in close order to the fire of an enemy that is not seen. It is evident that a few men scattered along and covered by a fence will successfully maintain their ground against an infinitely greater number drawn up in close order and remaining stationary in the middle of the field, for their fire is ineffectual, while every shot from the fence must strike a collected body . . . The skirmishers must avoid, too, as much as possible, remaining stationary in an open situation, but will gain ground from a flank under cover where it can be found, or, if necessary, advance to the front in extended line with as much rapidity as possible from one fence to another.

Graham thought that the Irish countryside provided the right conditions for this kind of tactic but the following year the regiment was on the move again, this time to the West Indies, where its station was at St Vincent in Barbados. During the posting in the Caribbean time did not sit heavily on the regiment's hands and the men were in regular action against French forces. The battles might have lacked the historic importance of the campaign in the peninsula, where Wellington was often outnumbered and had to make to do with the forces that he had and not with numbers that he might have wished, but the fighting was not without incident. For example, the 90th was involved in the capture of the French fort at Martinique on 2 February 1809 and with good reason the action was added to the regiment's battle honours, an honour shared with the 25th Foot (later The King's Own Scottish Borderers). During the operations the 90th was in the 2nd Division under the command of Major-General Frederick Maitland and his letter of thanks makes clear that the light-infantry training had paid dividends: 'The quickness with which they got under arms last night and had advanced is proof of the discipline of the regiment.'

This was followed in 1810 by the capture of the island of Guadeloupe, a more substantial prize as it contained a larger garrison. During the operations the 90th served in the third of five brigades and this contained the bulk of the light infantrymen. When the attack began on 29 January these were used as a diversion to the main assault and within a few days of sustained British fire-power white flags were flying over the French lines. This was followed by the surrender of the French garrisons on St Martin, St Eustatius and Saba, and the British were left as masters of the area. Later in the year the 90th returned to St Vincent where the commanding officer, Lieutenant-Colonel McNair, received orders to proceed to Canada. With him he took the thanks not only of the politicians in the local legislature but also of the island's association of merchants:

> It is a pleasing reflection that during a period of nearly nine years, such has been the harmony and friendship that have prevailed between every individual of the 90th Regiment and all ranks of the community, that no one solitary act of disagreement has occurred between them from their first arrival to the present day. Much as it may be attributed

to the well-known good order and military discipline of the regiment, they cannot fail to observe that it strongly marks its moral character, which, while it beams peace and harmony to its friends, makes it more to be feared by its enemy.

Quebec was to be the 90th's home until June 1815 when it returned to England. On arrival it discovered that it had been honoured with the official title of a light infantry regiment and was entitled to wear the rifle-green uniform of that corps which included the 13th (Somerset), 32nd (Duke of Cornwall's), 43rd (Monmouthshire), 51st (Yorkshire), 52nd (Oxfordshire), 53rd (Shropshire), 68th (Durham), 71st (Highland) and 85th (Buckinghamshire) light infantry regiments. In that guise it crossed over to France that summer to join the army of occupation following Napoleon's defeat at Waterloo on 18 June 1815. During the second stage of the war against Napoleon, following the failure of the Treaty of Amiens, the 90th had raised a 2nd battalion (not be confused with the earlier formation which had joined the Royal Marines) and this continued in service until it was disbanded in 1817. During its time it produced drafts for the 1st battalion. The regimental records of 1812 show that between them the two battalions were made up of 2,144 men consisting of 1,097 English, 538 Scots, 485 Irish and 24 foreigners, mainly Germans.

As for their colonel and founder Thomas Graham, his military career took him from operations in the Mediterranean to the Peninsula War where he was with Moore at Corunna and he played leading roles in the battles of Ciudad Rodrigo, Badajoz, Salamanca and Vittoria. In old age he retired to live in Scotland and London, and when in Edinburgh he was a regular visitor to the New Club. In his *Journal*, dated 24 October 1837, the distinguished judge and diarist Lord Cockburn gives an interesting sketch of the appearance of the gallant veteran after dining with Graham at the club the previous day:

> At the age of about eighty-eight [he was in fact ninety-one], his mind and body are both perfectly entire. He is still a great horseman, drives to London night and day in an open carriage, eats and drinks like an ordinary person, hears as well as others; sees well enough, after being operated upon, for all practical purposes, reading included; has the gallantry and politeness of an old soldier; enjoys and enlivens every company, especially where there are ladies, by a plain, manly, sensible, well-bred manner, and a conversation rich in his strong judgment, and with a memory full of the most interesting scenes and people of the last seventy years. Large in bone and feature, his head is finer than Jupiter's [the Rev. Alexander Carlyle]. It is like a grey, solid, war-worn castle. Nor has it only been in the affairs of war that his manly, chivalrous spirit has made him admired and loved. He has always taken a decided part in politics, on the popular side, and is one of the old Whigs, who find nothing good prevailing now but what he fought for and anticipated long ago. He is one of the men who make old age lovely.

Graham had been created Lord Lynedoch in May 1814 and died in London on 18 December 1843. His body was taken north by sea to Dundee and he was buried at Methven in Perthshire in the mausoleum that contained the remains of his wife, whose death had led indirectly to the formation of the 90th Perthshire Light Infantry.

FOUR

Crimea and the Indian Mutiny

In the middle of the nineteenth century the people of Britain faced two crises which struck at the heart of their confidence in the country's armed forces and the whole institution of empire. The first was the war against Russia, which was fought in the Crimea and the Baltic and in which Britain's allies were France, the Ottoman Empire and Sardinia; the second was the Indian Mutiny, which broke out in the Ganges Valley a year later. Neither was connected in any strategic sense but both rattled the harmony of Victorian life and led to widespread changes in the way the army was organised. Only the 90th Perthshire Light Infantry took part in both campaigns and it gained great distinction by winning eight Victoria Crosses, the new medal for supreme gallantry which was instituted by Queen Victoria in January 1856 to honour 'most conspicuous bravery, or some daring or pre-eminent act of valour or self-sacrifice or extreme devotion to duty' (see Appendix).

The Crimean War encompassed maladministration and human suffering on a grand scale; disaster marched hand in hand with heroism. It was also the first conflict to be fully covered by the press, most notably by William Howard Russell of *The Times*, and the reports from the front caused national outrage. For the British there was the heroic myth created by the Charge of the Light Brigade and the atonement offered by the example of Florence Nightingale and her gallant company of nurses in the infamous military hospital at Scutari. There was, though, more to the war than the oft-rehearsed catalogue of blunders redeemed by basic human courage and a refusal to surrender to overwhelming odds. For all the participants the war ended the long peace of 1815 and set in train the succession of small European conflicts and power struggles which dominated the second half of the nineteenth century and which led eventually to the global war of 1914–18.

The conflict had its starting point as a petty squabble between the Orthodox and Catholic churches over the rights to the holy sites in Jerusalem – the actual spark was possession of the key to the main door of the Church of the Nativity in Bethlehem – and quickly spread to become a war to prevent Russian expansionist ambitions in the Black Sea geo-strategic region. Tsar Nicholas I entertained hopes of using a perceived weakness of Ottoman rule to gain influence in the Balkans where there was a significant Slav population and began exerting diplomatic and military pressure on Constantinople. Matters escalated relentlessly and quickly brought the main participants to the verge of war. In the summer of 1853 Russian forces invaded the Ottoman Danubian principalities of Moldavia and Wallachia (modern Romania), a move which forced Turkey to declare war in October. From that point onwards a general conflict became inevitable as both Britain and France were opposed to the Russian moves and wished to shore up Ottoman rule. At the beginning of 1854, to great outrage in the rest of Europe, a Turkish naval squadron was overwhelmed and destroyed by the Russian fleet at Sinope and a few weeks later the British and French fleets sailed into the Black Sea followed by the mobilisation of both countries' land forces.

26TH CAMERONIAN REGIMENT OF FOOT

During the period between Waterloo and the Crimean War and the operations in India the 26th Cameronian Regiment was constantly on the move, with much of its time being spent in India and the Far East. It remained in Gibraltar until October 1821, when it returned to Ireland. This was a period when the first stirrings of agitation for Catholic emancipation had begun and while based at Fermoy the regiment had to provide constant patrols in support of the Irish police forces. A bigger problem, according to the records, was the need to protect the soldiers from the 'wretched moral condition of the lower orders in the towns, whose ignorance and profligacy rendered their society ruinous to all who kept it'. In this respect discipline was not helped by the fact that, as was common in those days, the regiment was broken up in several detachments scattered over a large area. Matters were improved by a supply of recruits from Scotland – 284 in the space of 14 months – who proved to be steady and disciplined soldiers. In the first half of 1827 the regiment received warning that its next posting would be India and permission was given for 12 wives per 100 men to make the long journey. Those selected (by ballot) were supposed to help as unofficial nurses and cooks, putting up with the same hardships endured by their husbands and the rest of the battalion. If their husbands died or were killed the usual practice was for the woman to marry another soldier in the regiment, usually within a day or so of being widowed. It was not a relationship for the squeamish and the army's official view was summed up by the editor of the *United Service Journal* at the beginning of the nineteenth century: 'the admission of females is an indulgence, contingent on their own conduct and usefulness and the due accommodation and recreations of the men'. In other words, if the wives wanted to be accepted by the regiment they had to make themselves useful. After a short posting at Chatham the regiment was transported to India in the spring of 1828 travelling aboard the troopships *Rose, Prince Regent, Asia* and *Marchioness of Ely.*

It was the regiment's first posting in a country which had a big influence on the British Army during the nineteenth century – some regiments remained in the country for up to 25 years and many men decided to stay on in India once their period of service had come to an end. Throughout the period British regiments were used to back up the forces of the East India Company in Bengal, Bombay and Madras and they bore the suffix HM before their regimental number to differentiate them from the presidency armies. On arrival in the latter station the Cameronian regiment was strengthened by the arrival of 234 rank and file from the 30th Foot (later 1st West Lancashire Regiment) and in 1830 it transferred to Bengal. During the next few months the regiment moved to Meerut and in so doing undertook 80 route marches which totalled 903 miles. The longest march was 16 miles and the shortest three. This was a period which the records described as 'undisturbed tranquillity' as the regiment settled down to the unfamiliar rhythms of service life in India, a country which the military historian Correlli Barnett has described as having provided 'the greatest formative influence on the life, language and legend of the British army . . . India, with its heat, stinks and noise, its enveloping dust, became the British army's second home – perhaps its first.' Due to the heat the day began early and parades and inspections were finished by nine o'clock with extra duties in the cool of later afternoon and evening. Those soldiers with wives on the strength generally enjoyed better conditions than they would at home – Indian servants were employed to help with domestic tasks – but for single men time could hang heavily on their hands.

Excessive drinking was a problem and, although the regimental records insist that everything was done to prevent the men from indulging in alcohol, an army return for 1833 shows that 710 men of the 26th managed to consume 5,320 gallons of arrack, 209 gallons of brandy, 249 gallons of gin and 5,175 gallons of beer. At the end of the year the regiment recorded 19 deaths and 50 other casualties from illness and discharges.

The period of enforced idleness came to an end at the beginning of 1840 when the regiment began preparations to move to China as part of the force which had been formed, according to the regimental records, 'in order that the ruling powers of the Celestial Empire might be taught to acknowledge the principles of international law, as understood by civilised nations'. This was the episode known as the First Opium War (1839–42), an undertaking which was later portrayed as a discreditable act of aggression but which at the time was considered to be a commendable piece of commercial and political opportunism. Having encouraged or at least connived at British merchants' importing opium, the Chinese authorities then took exception to the trade and started harassing them in a manner which attracted British retaliation. Under the command of Lieutenant-Colonel William James the 26th moved first to Singapore and then to Chusan where it took possession of the city of Tinghae. Almost immediately the regiment was ravaged by disease with the result that over 200 people had to be evacuated to Manila. By the end of the year the headquarters consisted of 273 officers and men, of whom 163 were counted as too sick to serve.

To begin with, operations were confined to the Canton River and the island of Hong Kong, which was annexed and would soon become a vital British naval base and commercial centre. A shortlived peace accord was signed but this did not hold and the British expeditionary force moved north to the Yangtse River with the intention of making a show of overwhelming force which would cow the Chinese, whose forces were armed with ancient matchlocks and a variety of bladed weapons. As a first stage the forts of Bocca Tigris and Howqua were reduced before moving to Canton, which fell at the end of the month. The 26th then operated in concert with the 37th Madras Native Infantry and the Bengal Volunteers under the overall command of Major-General Hugh Gough to engage the remaining Chinese forces in the nearby hills. The fighting was carried out in swampy conditions under a hot sun that was extremely debilitating for those involved. During the engagement the 26th lost three men killed (one to heatstroke) and 15 wounded. This was followed by the capture of Amoy, Tinghae, Chinchi and Ningpo, and at the end of the year the regiment was reinforced by a draft of 262 recruits from England. It also received its first Minié weapons, albeit in unrifled form so that the existing huge supply of musket balls would not be wasted. However, in its later form, the Minié rifle proved to be a major improvement on the 'wretched flintlock previously in use'.

In the next stage of the operations, during the spring of 1842, the 26th encountered sterner opposition in the shape of Tartar troops who not only fought with great stubbornness but preferred to commit suicide rather than surrender to the 'foreign devils', as they called the invading British forces. A contemporary account in the records of an incident at Chapoo gives some idea of the ferocity of the fighting:

> The rout of the Chinese soon became total, the fugitives throwing away their arms. At this period, three hundred tartars, finding their retreat cut off by Her Majesty's 26th Regiment, threw themselves into a loop-holed joss-house, in one of the defiles, and defended themselves a considerable time with most commendable bravery. The artillery had no effect in dislodging them. This check to the whole force

by a handful of men could not be borne, and several runs were made at the door to burst it in and get amongst them, but without effect. The gallant Colonel Tomlinson, of the 18th, was shot through the neck in leading one of these assaults, and several other officers and men fell at this spot. Ultimately, the place was fired by rockets, and breached by bags of powder, placed under the superintendence of Captain Pears, when about fifty of the defendants were taken prisoners, but nearly all of them wounded.

The end came in August with the capture of Chinkiang and Nanking, and the subsequent peace agreement imposed humiliating terms on the Chinese. Hong Kong was formally ceded to Britain and the treaty ports of Canton, Amoy, Foochow, Shanghai and Ningpo were opened to British trade. In commemoration of the part played by the regiment it was authorised to carry the word 'China' and the device of the 'Dragon' on the regimental colour and appointments. In February 1843 the 26th arrived back in Calcutta before returning to England in six transports. From Chatham it proceeded to Edinburgh and this was to be its home until the summer of 1845, when it moved once again to Ireland. After an uneventful posting the 26th sailed to Gibraltar in the summer of 1850. Its next station was Quebec in Canada, which was reached on 1 June 1851. This was followed by a move to Bermuda in the summer of 1854 when it was re-equipped with the new Enfield short rifle, a muzzle-loading rifled musket and the forerunner of later rifled personal weapons. The records describe it as 'a formidable weapon'. During the summer of 1859 the regiment's tour of duty came to an end and it returned to Ireland before moving to Glasgow two years later. Following a further period in the south of England the 26th sailed for India on 29 July 1865 under the command of Lieutenant-Colonel Shurlock

Henning. On arrival in Bombay the strength was 40 officers, 47 sergeants, 40 corporals, 19 drummers and 740 privates.

90TH PERTHSHIRE LIGHT INFANTRY

Four years after returning to England the 90th was warned for foreign service in September 1820 and moved first to Malta before proceeding to Cephalonia. This had come into British possession in 1815 as a result of the Treaty of Paris which had concluded the Napoleonic War and was ruled as the United States of the Ionian Islands with its capital on the island of Corfu, the seat of the British Lord High Commissioner. During the deployment the regiment was involved in a novel incident when a small detachment under the command of Lieutenant Wilson, formerly a Royal Navy officer, succeeded in capturing a notorious Greek pirate who had been terrorising the waters of the Ionian islands. In 1830 the 90th returned to Scotland before leaving for Ireland two years later. The companies were scattered over several different districts with the headquarters at Naas. Another overseas posting followed in 1836 when the regiment sailed for Ceylon (today Sri Lanka) where the main problem was combating the heat and humidity: 35 lives were lost to cholera and throughout the deployment there was a steady haemorrhage of men due to various illnesses. Following a ten-year tour of duty the 90th was relieved by the 15th Foot (later The East Yorkshire Regiment) and transferred to South Africa, but during the voyage disaster struck one of the transports, the *Maria Somes*, when it was overtaken by a hurricane-force storm. It raged for three days and 16 lives were lost, mainly from exhaustion or suffocation as a result of the hatches' being battened down. After carrying out repairs to the masts and rudder the *Maria Somes* eventually limped into Mauritius, where the survivors transferred to the transport *Mariner* and continued to Simonstown.

On arrival the regiment joined British forces engaged in fighting the Seventh Kaffir War, one of a series of nine conflicts with the Xhosa people, cattle-raising tribes of Eastern Natal which came about as the result of European expansionism as Dutch settlers began moving eastwards from the Cape in the 1770s. (In modern times the word 'kaffir' has acquired a pejorative meaning and the conflicts are now known as the Cape Frontier Wars.) The Seventh Kaffir War was also known as the War of the Axe because it was sparked by a Xhosa who murdered his escort while being taken to Grahamstown charged with stealing an axe. By the time the 90th arrived in South Africa most of the fighting was over but the regiment saw action with the 91st Foot (later 1st Argyll and Sutherland Highlanders) in the area between the Great Fish and Keiskamma rivers. At the beginning of 1847, with the conflict facing stalemate, the 90th was ordered to return to Britain only to find that the troopship had foundered before making landfall. As a result, the regiment remained in South Africa until the beginning of the following year. Before leaving, 100 men volunteered to remain in the country to join the Cape Mounted Rifles, which had been raised in 1827 to police the eastern frontier. In 1851 the 90th returned to Ireland and, three years later, it was based in Dublin when news arrived of the crisis in the Balkans and the Black Sea.

War had been declared at the beginning of April and command of the British expeditionary force was given to Lord Raglan, who as Lord Fitzroy Somerset had been Wellington's military secretary in the peninsula and who had an unblemished, if unspectacular, military career. His connection to Wellington counted for much, as did his personal courage (he lost his right arm at Waterloo) and his ability to get on with the French allies (he spoke fluent French but discommoded his allies in the Crimea by referring to them as 'the enemy'). The news that the British were to send an expeditionary force to the Black Sea was greeted with a widespread outburst of enthusiasm – *The Times* reported on 27 February that 'the prevalent feeling is an honourable and just one' and in the officers' mess of the 90th Lieutenant Nicol Graham from Ardrossan in Ayrshire wrote to his uncle in Portobello in Edinburgh expressing similar emotions:

> The 90th are as fine a looking corps as is in the service[.] they are all Perthshire men and a great many Grahams amongst them. The grenadiers are all six feet high & some of them six feet three & a half. No man in this Regiment is taken on under five feet ten. There is one Grahame in the Regt who is the strongest man in Dublin. He killed five men at Waterloo with his own hand & took two standards. In fact they are all as fine a set of men as you would wish to look at. It is supposed we will go Turkey where I am sure of promotion. I see from the papers that the English fleet has already set to work having taken several Russian ships. I should like to hear from you soon. I am drilled four hours a day & have to attend all court martials parades &c.

At the time the 90th was expecting orders to proceed to India but instead it was ordered to reinforce the British Army in the Crimea, travelling on board the troopship *Europa*, which reached Balaklava on 3 December 1854. On landing, the 90th joined 2 Brigade in the Light Division and immediately went into the trenches in front of Sevastopol, which had been under siege since the autumn. (The division's commander, Lieutenant-General Sir George Brown, was one of the most detested generals in the British Army: one subaltern called him 'an old imbecile bully'.) By then, following the battles of the Alma, Sevastopol and Inkerman, the war of manoeuvre had come to an end with the Russians holed up in Sevastopol and the allies entrenched outside. It was a precarious existence, with most of the casualties being caused by the extreme weather and the scandalous absence of the necessary equipment to counter the effects of a bitterly cold winter. Dr Douglas Arthur Reid joined the regiment in the Crimea in January 1855 and he quickly became aware that the prevailing conditions and the illness produced by them were the chief cause of casualties. His memoirs describe the predicament endured by everyone in the regiment:

> The extraordinary variableness of the Crimean climate in February was the cause of much distress and illness in the camp. In the early part of the month spring flowers were blooming in some of the ravines. I picked a crocus on the field of Inkerman, and violets and hyacinths were beginning to make a show. On the 21st I find in one of my notes that the thermometer was two degrees below zero and the camp buried in three feet of snow. It was difficult to get from one tent to another; our men were, many of them, badly frost-bitten. When I awoke in the morning my bed was covered with snow and ice and the floor of my tent was deep in snow. It was dreadful in the trenches at this time, and the men suffered terribly. For twenty-four hours at a stretch they were unable to lie down, the trenches being full of snow or water.
>
> It is not surprising that there was a lengthy sick list every morning.

At the same time, in the midst of the severe winter weather, the besieging forces kept up the pressure on the defenders by mounting attacks on their positions. One assault at the Gordon Battery, described by Garnet Wolseley, an officer in the 90th, will stand for many similar incidents during the period of the siege:

> With a loud 'hurrah', the gallant little band sprang with the bayonet upon the enemy, who at once precipitately retired over the parapet, followed by our rifle balls, which

were poured in upon them incessantly till every round in the men's pouches was expended. In order to keep up the fire, the men groped about among the dead Russians and exhausted all the cartridges they could find in the enemy's pouches.

On 10 September the 90th took part in one of several assaults on a heavily defended Russian position known as the Great Redan which was led by the 2nd Division and the Light Division with the Guards Division and the Highland Division in reserve. A huge artillery bombardment preceded the assault, which was led by storming parties drawn from 2 Brigade. Each group consisted of 100 men carrying ladders, 160 men (the 'forlorn hope') to make the initial assault and 500 men to follow up, with 100 in reserve. The second storming party included 300 men of the 90th under the command of Captain R. Grove. As the British infantry crossed the open ground of the salient they encountered heavy Russian artillery and rifle fire but they pressed home their attack and managed to enter the Redan where the fight continued at bayonet point. This was the last set-piece battle of the war and the Russians responded to the allied assault by pulling out of Sevastopol leaving behind their wounded and many of their stores. The fighting which produced the breakthrough was witnessed and later described by William Howard Russell, the distinguished war correspondent of *The Times* whose revelations did so much to change public attitudes towards the war and the incompetence shown by the government and senior army officers:

> Our soldiers, taken at every disadvantage, met the enemy with the bayonet too, and isolated combats occurred, in which the brave fellows who stood their ground had to defend themselves against three or four adversaries at once. In this melee, the officers, armed only with their swords,

had little chance; nor had those who carried pistols much opportunity of using them in such a close and sudden contest. They fell like heroes, and many a gallant soldier with them. The bodies of the English and Russians inside the Redan, locked in an embrace which death could not relax, but had rather cemented all the closer, were found next day as evidence of the terrible animosity of the struggle.

The battle lasted just under two hours and during that time the 90th lost four officers and four rank and file killed, 12 officers and 132 rank and file wounded. Four sergeants and 33 privates were posted as missing. Ahead lay another winter in the field and it was not until the following spring that peace talks brought the war to an end, but most of the long-suffering regiments, including the 90th, were not sent home until June 1856. As was the case with most regiments which served in the Crimea, the bulk of the casualties succumbed not to enemy fire but to the privations of disease caused by the harsh conditions. In the church of St Swithun's in East Grinstead a memorial plaque tells the bleak story of one of the regiment's casualties: 'Robert Henry Crawford Capt. in HM 90th Light Infantry eldest son of Robert Crawford of Saint Hill. Died February 24th 1855 at Scutari of fever brought on by hardship and exposure during the disastrous winter campaign before Sebastopol aged 30 years.'

On its arrival in England the 90th moved to Aldershot, where it remained until February 1857 when it moved again, this time to Portsmouth. The regiment had only been at Anglesea Barracks for a week when it received orders to proceed immediately to India. A few weeks later the deployment was changed to China and at the beginning of April the regiment set sail in two transports, the *Himalaya* and the *Transit*. After calling in at Cape Town the *Himalaya* was intercepted by a frigate of the Royal Navy and ordered to make speed for Calcutta as a result of a serious outbreak of violence in India involving Indian regiments of the East India Company's Bengal Army which rapidly escalated to threaten the whole fabric of British rule. On 10 May 1857 the uprising known as the Indian (or Sepoy) Mutiny had begun at Meerut, where the 11th and 20th Native Infantry and 3rd Cavalry regiments rose up against the local European population and started slaughtering them. The trouble had been simmering throughout the year and, amongst other grievances, the flashpoint was the decision to issue Indian troops with cartridges using the grease of pigs and cows, offending both Muslims (who regard pigs as unclean) and Hindus (for whom cows are sacred). The trouble spread to other British garrisons at Cawnpore, where the garrison was slaughtered on 27 June despite promises of safe conduct, and at Lucknow where the European population was besieged in the Residency by a force of 60,000 mutineers.

No sooner had the men of the 90th disembarked from the *Himalaya* on 21 July than they were sent by river steamers to move up the Ganges to Allahabad and Berhampore. Their first task was to disarm the 63rd Native Infantry and 11th Irregular Cavalry, and this was executed without loss of life, although the regimental records noted that the Bengali troops 'manifested the utmost dissatisfaction' at what was being done to them. From there the regiment was sent to join the forces under the command of Major-General James Outram, who intended to support Brigadier-General Henry Havelock in the operations to relieve Lucknow. On arrival at Cawnpore on 15 September the regiment was brigaded with 78th Highlanders (later 2nd Seaforth Highlanders) and the Ferozepore Regiment. Although senior in rank Outram waived the right to lead the reinforced column, by then 3,000-strong, so that Havelock could complete what he had begun. On 19 September the force set off and two days later the 78th and the 90th successfully cleared the village of Mangalwar with a spirited bayonet charge. During the operation one of the 90th's casualties was Private John Alexander, who had been gazetted in the Crimea for the award of the Victoria Cross but had not yet received the medal.

Despite the onset of heavy rain the advance continued apace and three days later Lucknow was finally in sight. Havelock ordered that the main assault should be made on 25 September and over two days of heavy fighting the relieving force fought its way into the Residency. While this was happening Surgeon Anthony Home of the 90th was left with a party of wounded protected only by a handful of riflemen who quickly attracted the attention of the mutineers. Despite keeping up heavy fire on the attackers their situation quickly deteriorated and an acute shortage of fresh water added to their discomfort. As Home wrote later in the regimental records, he and the men under his care had given themselves up to despair and decided on a final gamble:

> I proposed to the men either to force our way back to the rear-guard, or forward to the Residency. They agreed, but on creeping forward, under shadow of the building, I found a large fire burning in the archway, and great numbers of men clustered about it. Escape, that way, was utterly impossible, whilst by the way by which we had come, we had to rush through the men who had just successfully repelled our own soldiers. To escape and carry away the wounded was hopeless. We resigned ourselves completely to our fate. A little after day-break, we were roused by distant firing. This time it had no effect upon us. It, however, approached nearer and nearer, then [Private] Ryan, suddenly jumping up, shouted, 'Oh boys! Them's our own chaps!' We then all united in a cheer, and kept shouting to keep them on their right.

For his courage and leadership Home was awarded the Victoria Cross, as was his colleague Assistant-Surgeon William Bradshaw, also of the 90th. Later in his career Home was knighted and was appointed Surgeon-General.

Although Havelock's column had managed to fight its way into Lucknow it had not raised the siege and now found that it too was in peril. Lacking the necessary transport and depleted in size due to the heavy casualties, the relieving force could neither escort the civilians out of Lucknow nor hope to engage the superior numbers of besieging mutineers. In short, the rescuers were now the besieged. To add to the problems, conditions inside Lucknow began to deteriorate, soldiers were put on half rations and their uniforms were in tatters. A particular menace was the number of mines dug by the Indians besieging the city: 21 shafts were discovered, some them 200 feet in depth.

Fortunately, help was on its way. Fresh from his exploits in the Crimea, where he had commanded the Highland Division, Lieutenant-General Sir Colin Campbell had been appointed commander-in-chief of the forces in India and had made the relief of Lucknow his main priority. On 12 November he arrived at the Alam Bagh outside the city with a force of around 700 cavalry and 2,700 infantry and was able to enter the beleaguered Residency a week later. Once again, though, the relieving force was too small to hold the place and Campbell decided to withdraw his forces and establish a new defensive position at the Alam Bagh. By then the remaining three companies of the regiment from the troopship *Transit* had finally reached India and the 90th took part in the final operations to capture the vital Sikandarbagh, a fortified garden position which had to be taken before the attack could continue. The main assault was undertaken by the 53rd Foot, 93rd Highlanders and the 4th Punjab Infantry. During the fighting Campbell's force lost 45 officers and 496 soldiers.

The next stage was to remove the women and children from the Residency compound, which was achieved on 24 November, and Outram's force of 4,000 occupied the Alam Bagh while Campbell removed the rump of the army to Cawnpore. (Havelock succumbed to illness that same day and died in his son's arms after telling him, 'Harry, see how a Christian can die.') Lucknow remained in rebel hands until March the following year when the 90th was part of the force which captured La Martinière College and the Sikandarbagh. Three days later, 14 March 1858, six companies of the regiment attacked and captured the Kesar (or Kaiser) Bagh palace. Although many of the mutineers had drifted off to the surrounding countryside, the regimental records make clear that the mopping-up operations still produced dangers and difficulties:

> The day was one of long and continued exertion, and everyone felt that, although much remained to be done before the final expulsion of the rebels, the most difficult part had been overcome. The 15th [March] was employed in securing what had been taken, removing powder, destroying mines, and fixing mortars for future bombardment of the positions still held by the enemy on the line of our advance up the right bank of the Goomtee [River Gumti], and in the heart of the city.

Lucknow finally fell a week later and in one of the final attacks the 90th joined forces with the 14th Ferozepore Sikhs to storm the mutineers' positions. In the regimental history Major Jeremiah Brasyer of the latter regiment produced a graphic account of the difficulties faced by the stormers as they rushed into the well-defended position of the Kesar Bagh:

> The men were excited and eager to go on. Without orders, my Sikhs like monkeys climbed a wall and opened a large

gate which gave outlet from the smaller Emambarra, while I, with other officers, joined them. A rush such as nothing could stop followed. The General [Thomas Franks] smiled as he cheered my men, but issued no order. This acquiescence was enough, I knew what he wanted. My Sikhs like greyhounds let loose, passed into the street, deafening cheers encouraged us, while the General and his staff followed in support. We rushed onwards, cleared 40 guns in battery en route, driving all before us. Pickaxe and shovel were next at work, and soon a breach was opened in an outer wall.

With the final capture of Lucknow the fighting against the remaining mutineers entered a new phase and for the rest of the year the 90th was involved in operations to subdue the last outposts of discontent in Oudh. After the mutiny was over the regiment commemorated its casualties on a memorial plaque which was placed on a wall of the ruined Residency building in Lucknow:

Erected by the officers of H.M. 90 Light Infantry in memory of their comrades who fell during the Indian Rebellion of 1857 & 1858 and as a tribute to their gallantry. Colonel Robert P. Campbell C.B. died of his wounds at Lucknow 12th November 1857. Major Roger Barnston died of his wounds at Cawnpore 23rd December 1857. Brevet Major James Perrin died of his wounds at Alumbagh 30th September 1857.

Captain Harry Denison died of his wounds at Lucknow 29th October 1857. Lieutenant Nicol Graham killed in action at Alumbagh 23rd Sept 1857. Lieutenant John Joshua Nunn killed in action at Alumbagh 24th Sept 1857. Lieutenant Arthur Moultrie killed in action at Lucknow 26th September 1857. Lieutenant W.H.L.

Carleton died of small pox at Lucknow 10th April 1858. Lieutenant R.G. Synce died of consumption at Lucknow 8th September 1858. Lieutenant N. Preston died of his wounds at Alumbagh 27th September 1857. Ensign Arthur Chute died of dyssentry at Calcutta 23rd February 1858. Ensign Hugh Gordon died of coup de soleil [heat stroke] at Lucknow 28th May 1858. Assistant Surgeon R. Nelson died of fever 18th August 1857. Also to the memory of 271 non-commissioned officers and privates of the Regiment who fell in the gallant performance of their duty at the Relief the Defence and the Capture of Lucknow and during the subsequent campaign in Oudh.

Of those casualties of the 90th Perthshire Light Infantry, Lieutenant Preston was the son of the Rev. W. M. S. Preston of Warcop Hall in Westmoreland; his brother Henry had already been killed in the Crimea. Harry Denison had his arm amputated after being wounded on 6 October 1857 and died of septicaemia three weeks later. Of the other casualties listed on the memorial plaque, Nicol Graham was the young officer who had written so fulsomely to his uncle before the regiment departed for India, and Major and Brevet Lieutenant-Colonel Barnston had been appointed CB for his leadership in the Crimea. India was to be the regiment's home until 1869 when it returned to Britain; by then it had been on foreign service for 13 years.

FIVE

The Late Victorian Army

In the aftermath of the Crimean War the War Office instituted a number of reforms to improve the lot of the British soldier. Changes were also made to the operation and structure of the army but given the prevailing conservatism many of the proposed reforms took time to take root. A Staff College came into being at Camberley to provide further intensive training for promising officers, the Crimean conflict having exposed the weakness of reliance on regimental soldiering alone. Recruitment problems were addressed by introducing short-service enlistment, the number of years being reduced from 21 years to six years with the Colours and six in the Reserves. As for the purchase of officers' commissions, which had been much criticised during the war, the system was not abolished until 1871. Although the new system made entry to the army and subsequent promotion dependent on merit, it did not make much material difference to the social backgrounds of the officers, who continued to come from the upper and middle classes. Had it been in place earlier in the century it would also have deprived the regiment of Henry Evelyn Wood, one of its most distinguished soldiers, who was awarded the Victoria Cross during the Indian Mutiny while serving with 17th Light Dragoons. Originally a midshipman in the Royal Navy, he transferred to the 13th Light Dragoons and served variously with the 73rd Foot (later 2nd Black Watch) and 17th Foot (later The Royal Leicestershire Regiment) before purchasing his majority in the 90th Perthshire Light Infantry. Later in his career he was appointed sirdar (commander) of the Egyptian Army and was promoted field marshal in 1903.

Another notable officer from this period was Garnet Wolseley, whom we have already met in the Crimea. A future field marshal, he was born in Dublin in 1833, the son of an officer in the 25th Foot (later The King's Own Scottish Borderers); having purchased his commission in the 12th Foot (later The Suffolk Regiment) in 1852 his first soldiering was spent with the 80th Foot (later 2nd North Staffordshire Regiment), which was serving in India. After seeing action in the Second Burma War Wolseley transferred to the 90th Perthshire Light Infantry in 1854 and served with them in the Crimean War and during the Indian Mutiny. His early experiences in the army did not enamour him of the system of officer selection and while he accepted that there should be a high premium on personal courage he later wrote in his memoirs that most of the officers of his period were uninterested in theory or tactics and were incapable of fighting modern wars:

> Almost all our officers at that time were uneducated as soldiers, and many of those placed upon the staff of the Army at the beginning of the [Crimean] war were absolutely unfit for the positions they had secured through family and political interest ... they were not men I would have trusted with a subaltern's picket in the field. Had they been private soldiers, I don't think any colonel would have made them corporals.

In 1869 Wolseley published *The Soldier's Pocket Book for Field Service*, which became the standard military textbook of its day with its insistence on the need for thorough and painstaking preparation before undertaking any operation. Not for nothing was the phrase 'All Sir Garnet' a byword for efficiency and good practice. Later he was promoted field marshal and in 1895 became commander-in-chief of the British Army, succeeding his great rival, the deeply conservative Duke of Cambridge. As Wolseley climbed up the army lists he made a point of personally selecting his officers and nurturing military talent. In time the officers who served with him would be known as the 'Wolseley Ring' and once they had come to his notice their careers usually prospered. However, for all that he became one of the great commanders of the nineteenth century, he never lost his affection for the 90th Perthshire Light Infantry and was to write of them affectionately in his memoirs:

> Amongst the officers of my regiment, nice fellows as they were, only a few cared much for the Army as a profession. All were proud of belonging to a splendidly drilled Light Infantry Battalion – drilled according to the practice of War in the Peninsula, before the introduction of a rifled musket. They thought themselves socially superior to the ordinary regiments of the Line, which were always spoken of as 'grabbies'. Many of them were well connected, and some were well off. It was in every respect a home for gentlemen, and in that respect much above the great bulk of line regiments.

To understand Wolseley's comments, there was an unofficial pecking order amongst the regiments of the British Army. At the peak were the cavalry regiments and the foot guards followed in no particular order by the rifle regiments, the light infantry and the Highland infantry regiments. Whatever the regiment, though, every officer was expected to have a private income as the annual pay of a second lieutenant, the entry rank, was just over £95 a year (£6,500 today) and that was insufficient to cover his uniform costs and mess bills, which amounted to roughly £10 a month. As late as 1914 the War Office recommended that the minimum needed to survive was £160 a year (£11,000 today) but even that amount meant that a young officer would have to lead an abstemious existence. Some regiments were extremely expensive. Officers in cavalry or foot guards regiments had to purchase a variety of uniforms to meet all the variations in service and mess dress; they were expected to live well in the mess and to keep at least two hunters and three polo ponies. In the late Victorian and Edwardian periods it was not considered unusual for a smart cavalry regiment to insist on a young officer being in possession of a private income of up to £1,000 a year (£68,000 today). For the Scottish regiments this made the Royal Scots Greys and the Scots Guards the most expensive, but smarter Highland regiments such as The Black Watch or Queen's Own Cameron Highlanders required a private income close to £400 a year (£27,500 today). Lowland regiments such as the 26th were a little less costly at an average of £250 a year (£17,000 today) and the implied differences in social scale were not only understood but accepted by the men involved. So too were the differences in rank within a battalion. Officers were meant to be a breed apart but they were also supposed to put their men's best interests before theirs and prided themselves on setting high personal standards of behaviour.

On the equipment side the first breech-loading rifles were introduced in 1868 (the Snider followed by the Martini-Henry and the Enfield) but the army's traditional red coats were not replaced by khaki until the 1880s, when campaigning in the deserts of Egypt and Sudan made ceremonial dress inappropriate for operational service. (The change to khaki was gradual and was not made official until 1902.) In appearance the regiments in the Crimea looked remarkably similar to their forebears in the peninsula. One other major change only affected the Highland regiments: in 1854 the War Office finally sanctioned the official employment of a pipe-major and five pipers. Previously they had been listed as drummers in order to receive the additional extra-duty pay of one penny a day; the ruling did not apply to non-Highland regiments or to the Lowland regiments, where the the expense of clothing and maintaining pipers was borne by the officers' mess, and they were distributed throughout the regiment disguised on the muster roll as 'drummers'. Pipers had been present in the 26th and the 90th before 1881 (in the former's case as early as 1713) when both battalions had pipes and drums in addition to the military band. The matter was raised by the War Office in June 1862 and the commanding officer of the 26th was obliged to admit that 'no trace of the original authority or date of their formation exists'. Wisely the War Office let the matter drop. In later years the pipers in the 2nd battalion adopted grey sporrans with three black tassels to differentiate them from the 1st battalion pipers who wore a black sporran with two white tassels, and their kilts were of Douglas tartan.

The terrible conditions endured by the army also encouraged a flurry of interest in soldiers' welfare. In 1857 a Royal Sanitary Commission investigated the conditions in barracks and military hospitals and its findings merely underlined the nation's low opinion of its armed forces. The mortality rate amongst soldiers was double that of the civilian population, with the home-based army losing 20.8 per cent of its strength due to illness or disease. The Commissioners placed the blame on unsanitary conditions, poor diet and the 'enervating mental and bodily effects produced by ennui'. Their recommendations led to a steady improvement in the soldier's lot: a programme was instituted to improve ventilation, sanitary conditions and waste disposal in British barracks, and steps were taken to provide soldiers with better leisure facilities in an attempt to cut down on the scourge of drunkenness. Two years later parliament voted £726,841 for the improvements, but the reforms proved to be a slow and expensive process and it was to take until 1861 before the Commission on Barracks and Hospitals could report that 45 barracks had proper lavatories in place of the usual cesspits which had been there for generations.

The mutiny in India also prompted reform: in its aftermath steps were taken to increase the size of the garrison in the sub-continent to ensure that the Indian army of 190,000 soldiers was balanced by the presence of 80,000 British soldiers. For the next 60 years Britain was to play no part in the wars which were fought in Europe, the main conflict being the Franco–Prussian War of 1871. Instead, the army was to spend most of its time engaged in colonial policing duties in various parts of Britain's imperial holdings. The 26th and the 90th were both part of that process.

26TH CAMERONIAN REGIMENT OF FOOT

In late October 1865 the transports carrying the 26th arrived in Bombay, where the regiment formed part of the Belgaum Brigade under the command of Brigadier-General A.T. Heyland. India was the regiment's home until 1875 and during the tour it built up an enviable reputation for its skill at shooting, coming first in the army's classification tests in 1874. Shortly after arriving it also added to its battle honours by taking part in the shortlived Abyssinian War of 1867, when it served under Lieutenant-General Sir Robert Napier, the commander of the forces of the Bombay Presidency. This conflict came about as a result of the bizarre behaviour of the Emperor Theodore, who imprisoned several Europeans including the British consular agent, a move which prompted a huge relief force numbering 64,000 to invade the country and march on the main Abyssinian stronghold at Magdala. Although the 26th was in reserve during the attack, the regimental history recorded the unusual fact that 'a battle honour had been won without casualties'. On returning to Britain the 26th was stationed variously in Glasgow, Aldershot and Chatham before moving to Malta. It was a time of great change in the structure of the infantry and the first radical reorganisation since the abolition of colonels' names in 1751 and the introduction of numbering. The new scheme affected the 26th as well as the 90th.

For some time the War Office had toyed with the idea of introducing a territorial system by which every regiment would be linked to its own local recruiting area. The result was the creation of Sub-District Brigade Depots which paired 141 infantry battalions at 69 brigade depots. Under this scheme in 1873 the 26th was linked with 74th Highlanders (later 2nd Highland Light Infantry) at No. 59 Brigade Depot at Hamilton. At the same time the 90th was linked with 73rd Highlanders (later 2nd Black Watch) at No. 60 Depot, also at Hamilton. Neither pairing was entirely logical. From a historical point of view the history and traditions of the 26th, a Lowland regiment with a Covenanting background, were completely different from the 74th, which had been raised in 1787 as a Highland regiment. Equally, the 90th was a light infantry regiment, albeit raised originally in Perthshire, while the 73rd had also been raised as a Highland regiment. The new shared depot would also be home to two militia battalions and to five battalions of the Lanarkshire Rifle Volunteers which eventually formed the basis of The Cameronians Territorial Force battalions (see below).

However, further change was in the air. At the time all infantry regiments numbered 1st to 25th and the two Rifle Brigade regiments (60th and 95th) had multiple battalions and plans were now prepared to provide all regiments with two battalions through a process of amalgamation. Under a process begun in 1872 under the direction of the Secretary for War, Edward Cardwell, and finalised nine years later by his successor, Hugh Childers, the remaining single-battalion regiments were linked with others of their kind to form new two-battalion regiments and provided with territorial designations. Under this refinement the 26th joined forces with the 90th to form a new two-battalion regiment to be known initially as The Scotch Rifles (Cameronians). Within a year this was changed to the more accurate and less cumbersome title The Cameronians (Scottish Rifles), Queen Victoria having expressed a wish that the word 'Scotch' should not be used. Driving the Cardwell/Childers reforms was the theory that one battalion would serve at home while the other was stationed abroad and would receive drafts and reliefs from the home-based battalion to keep it up to strength. As a result of the localisation changes regimental numbers were dropped and territorial names were adopted throughout the army but, as happens in every period of reform, the changes outraged older soldiers, who deplored the loss of cherished numbers and the introduction of what they held to be undignified territorial names, some of which bore no relation to the new regiment's traditions and customs. For example, the 26th had to surrender its colours because rifle regiments do not carry them and these were laid up in Glasgow Cathedral on 9 July 1885.

However, at the time the combination of the two regiments was reasonably harmonious, as it proved possible to incorporate each regiment's history and traditions in the new formation. It helped the feelings of the 90th that it was becoming part of a Rifle regiment, thought at the time to be socially superior to a heavy marching regiment such as the 26th (see Wolseley's comments, above) although, as Philip Grant has proved in his history of the formation of the regiment, the 'Rifles' appellation was originally given to the 26th largely as a result of its well-known proficiency at shooting. For a long time, though, the two battalions continued to use different titles. The 1st battalion always referred to itself as

'Cameronians' while the 2nd battalion tended to use 'Scottish Rifles', and as John Baynes explained in his history of the latter battalion during the First World War, there was a good deal of rivalry, not all of it friendly, between the two battalions:

> The trouble sprang from the fact that the 90th considered themselves in every way vastly superior to the 26th. The officers were conscious of social superiority, and the men of the distinction of being in the Light Infantry. For all ranks the amalgamation with a rather dull, heavyfooted 'marching' regiment like the 26th was most distressing. Unfortunately the 26th thought rather a lot of themselves as well; they were a hundred years older than the 90th, had been raised by the Earl of Angus, a member of the Duke of Hamilton's family, and they had one of the finest fighting records of any infantry regiment of the British Army.

Even as late as 1914 the arrival of a new commanding officer from the 1st battalion was enough to upset feelings within the officers' mess of the 2nd battalion and the differences between the two battalions did not really disappear until after the First World War.

90TH PERTHSHIRE LIGHT INFANTRY

The regiment returned to Britain in the autumn of 1869 travelling on board HMS *Jumna* to Suez before continuing the journey by rail to Alexandria, where it boarded HMS *Serapis* bound for Portsmouth. At the end of the year it moved to Edinburgh, where it took up residence in the castle with one company stationed at Greenlaw in Berwickshire. Its strength was 27 officers, five staff, 49 sergeants, 20 buglers, 40 corporals and 520 private soldiers. Three companies were detached to Stirling castle while two companies went to Ayr and one to Dundee.

The next move was overseas: in September 1873 the 90th renewed its connection with Garnet Wolseley. By then a rising star in the upper echelons of the British Army, Wolseley had been given command of a task force charged with bringing law and order to the coastal people of the Gold Coast in west Africa, who were being attacked by an inland tribe, the Ashanti, led by King Kofi Karikari (whom the British soldiers immediately christened 'King Coffee'). As the tribes on the coast were under British protection the government decided to send a military force to the region to punish the Ashanti and put an end to their depredations. During the operation the regiment was commanded by Lieutenant-Colonel Evelyn Wood VC.

The main problem facing the British forces was the local topography. Beyond the coastal regions there were no roads and tracks had to be created through the dense bush where there were very few paths. To complicate matters, many of the local porters deserted, forcing the British soldiers to carry their own equipment, a difficult task given the fact that they would shortly be going into action against a tough enemy. The advance guard was under the command of Colonel McLeod of the 42nd Royal Highlanders and they were first to make contact with the enemy at the town of Amoaful where thousands of Ashanti had assembled to give battle. As was the case in so many of the punitive wars which were fought during Queen Victoria's reign, the ensuing battle was savagely unequal. While the Ashanti had superior numbers and demonstrated raw courage, they lacked modern weapons and their bullets were little more than lead slugs. Against them the British forces, drawn up in four columns, were well trained and possessed the modern breech-loading Martini-Henry rifle with a .45-inch calibre described by contemporaries as 'a real man-stopper'. That being said, the fighting at Amoaful proved hard going, especially on the right flank where Wood's men had to fight in dense bush.

British casualties were four killed and 194 wounded; amongst them were Lieutenant T. A. Eyre, the 90th's adjutant. (In Wood's autobiography there is a touching sketch of him attending Eyre after the 'gallant boy' had been 'shot through the body when showing a grand example to his men'.)

The Ashanti had been defeated but that did not encourage them to surrender. On the contrary, they continued to attack Wolseley's supply columns and the British force had to push deeper into Ashanti territory. The end came at Ordahsu outside their capital Kumasi, where they made their last stand in a battle which captured headlines all over the world. Following the engagement the British forces entered Kumasi to find it deserted as King Kofi and his followers had escaped, taking with them most of the treasure which Wolseley hoped to find. Having packed up what remained into carriers, Wolseley's men then blew up the main buildings and set fire to the rest of Kumasi, razing it to the ground. Shortly afterwards King Kofi entered into a peace agreement with the British, recognising them as the main power in the Gold Coast and promising to keep the peace in return for trading agreements.

At the end of the Ashanti War the regiment was based first at Aldershot and then in Ireland before proceeding on operational service in South Africa in 1878. Once again the area was in a state of turmoil following the rapid economic expansion of Cape Colony in the previous decade – diamonds had been discovered in Griqualand and this had attracted fresh investment, a new wave of immigrants and a need to develop the infrastructure. As white expansionism increased there was also a need to maintain a passive black African population, but, far from acquiescing, there were outbreaks of unrest amongst the native Griquas, the Xhosa and the Pedi and Basotho in Transvaal. These were put down by the superior firepower of the British garrison but to the colonial administration the main threat seemed to come from King Cetshwayo (or Cetewayo) of the Zulu nation and war quickly became inevitable. In a cynical piece of political manoeuvring Cetshwayo was provoked into attacking and destroying a column of 1,200 British troops and African auxiliaries at Isandlwana on 20 January 1879. Although the defeat seemed to be redeemed by the heroic stand of a small outpost at Rorke's Drift a few days later, British public opinion was outraged by the setback and there was a widespread thirst for revenge.

Fortunately, the 90th was not present at Isandlwana, being employed elsewhere in Wood's Number 4 column together with 13th Light Infantry, the Frontier Light Horse and four guns of 11th Battery, 7 Brigade, Royal Artillery. Following the defeat at Isandlwana, Lord Chelmsford, the British commander-in-chief, had regrouped his forces in Natal, a smaller column under the command of Colonel C. K. Pearson was under siege in a mission station at Eshowe in southern Zululand while Wood's Number 4 column operated to the north. This latter force scored a spectacular if one-sided success at Khambula on 29 March when the superior firepower of Wood's column accounted for the deaths of 3,000 Zulus armed only with spears and ancient muskets. The British losses tell their own story: 18 killed and 57 wounded. An accompanying correspondent from *The Times* described what happened when two companies of the 90th under the command of Major R. F. Hackett joined the battle to relieve pressure on the 13th, which was defending the force's cattle park:

> I watched Major Hackett leading his men, with his pipe in his mouth, as cool and collected as man could be; he gallantly advanced over the ridge, where his men lay down and opened fire on the Zulus who were now under the wagons of the cattle laager. Almost at once the enfilade fire began to tell. A Colour-Sergeant was shot through the head and other casualties occurred in quick succession.

Encouraged by the victory, Chelmsford decided to march quickly to relieve Pearson's force at Eshowe, splitting his force into two divisions which numbered 3,390 British soldiers and 2,280 African auxiliaries. In a local reorganisation Wood's force became the Flying Column and took part in the operations which culminated in the defeat of Cetshwayo's army at Ulundi in the middle of July. On 20 October 1879 the 90th left South Africa on board HMS *Serapis*; ahead lay the amalgamation with the 26th as part of the Cardwell/ Childers reforms of the structure of the infantry (see above).

1ST CAMERONIANS (SCOTTISH RIFLES)

Following the amalgamation 1st Cameronians remained in Britain as the home service battalion being garrisoned at Shorncliffe before moving back to Glasgow in 1884. Ireland and England were to be its home until 1894, when it exchanged roles with the 2nd battalion and moved to India, its first home being Rhaniket. This was followed by postings to Lucknow, Nowshera and Cawnpore during the heyday of the British Raj. When Rory Baynes joined the battalion in Cawnpore he found constant echoes of the writings of Rudyard Kipling and, like many young officers, most of what he learned came from the senior non-commissioned officers. At the time the battalion consisted of eight rifle companies and training was left in the hands of the subalterns. Baynes also discovered he had to sign a pledge promising to pay a fine of £50 if he married before reaching the rank of captain and he learned the important lesson that following route marches no officer was allowed to remove any of his kit or drink water until he made sure that his men had settled down and had received their own food and drink. Social life centred on the civilian club and for the officers there was duck shooting and polo. In 1909 the battalion moved to South Africa to relieve 2nd Argyll and Sutherland Highlanders and three years later it was back in Glasgow, where it remained until the outbreak of the First World War. Some idea of the financial problems facing young officers in the pre-First World War period can be found in Baynes's experience. While, as we have seen, The Cameronians was not considered a particularly expensive regiment, Baynes found mess life in a home station to be a drain on his finances and in 1912 he applied to join the Royal West African Frontier Force, where costs were lower and the pay went further.

2ND CAMERONIANS (SCOTTISH RIFLES)

For the first years of its existence 2nd Scottish Rifles was based in India, which was to be its home until 1895. The efficacy of the new scheme allowed it to be reinforced by regular drafts from 1st Cameronians; by then, too, one of its officers, Lieutenant-Colonel J. H. Laye, had been transferred to command the 1st battalion, a sign of things to come. On returning to Britain the battalion served in England and Ireland before moving to Glasgow in the autumn of 1899. It was the calm before the storm. On 12 October war broke out in South Africa, where the Boers of Transvaal and Orange Free State had invaded neighbouring Natal. Britain had been at loggerheads with the Boers – Dutch immigrants who had settled in Cape Colony – for most of the century. The fuse was provided in 1886 by the discovery of seemingly limitless supplies of gold in Boer territory south of Pretoria and the lure of untold riches attracted speculators from Britain and all over Europe. Before long the Boers were outnumbered by outsiders who threatened their traditional conservative way of life, and to protect his fellow Boers in the Transvaal President Kruger passed stringent laws excluding non-Boers from participation in political life while retaining the right to tax them. Such a state of affairs was bound to cause trouble and with two peoples unable to find an accommodation in order to live together war was perhaps inevitable.

On leaving for the battle front 2nd Scottish Rifles formed 4 Brigade in 2nd Division, being brigaded with 3rd King's Royal Rifle Corps, 1st Durham Light Infantry and 1st Rifle Brigade, all under the command of Major-General the Hon. N. G. Lyttelton. The battalion's strength was 25 officers and 936 men and it left for South Africa on 28 October, reaching Durban three weeks later. In the initial stages of the campaign the battalion saw little action but it was in the country when the army suffered the agonies of three consecutive defeats during December, a period which the war correspondent Arthur Conan Doyle christened 'Black Week' (these were Stormberg, Magersfontein and Colenso). As a result of the setback command of the army was given to Lord Roberts VC, a veteran of the Indian Mutiny and the fighting in Afghanistan, while his chief of staff was Lord Kitchener, who had inflicted a decisive defeat on Islamic fundamentalists in Sudan at the Battle of Omdurman in September 1898. This left the Scottish Rifles in Natal, where the battalion formed part of the relief force led by General Sir Redvers Buller VC to raise the Boers' siege of Ladysmith. Due to tardy planning and indecisive leadership the advance was so slow that the Boers had little difficulty in guessing the British intentions and the result was another setback.

On the night of 23/24 January 1900 the battalion was part of a force which occupied a bridgehead on the northern bank of the River Tugela while another force, 2,000-strong, had been deployed on the flat top of Spion Kop, a rocky outcrop overlooking the river. Following a determined and largely successful Boer attack to dislodge the British from the summit the Scottish Rifles was ordered to make haste for the summit supported by troopers of Bethune's Mounted Infantry. Despite coming under heavy fire a gallant bayonet charge cleared the enemy positions and the Boers retreated. In the aftermath the British also found the position untenable and began to withdraw, having suffered over 1,000 casualties. By 4.30 a.m. both sides had fought themselves to a standstill and when Conan Doyle and other war correspondents arrived at the summit they found scenes of chaos:

> As the shades of night closed in, and the glare of the bursting shells became more lurid, the men lay extended upon the rocky ground, parched and exhausted . . . Twelve hours of so terrible an experience had had a strange effect upon many of the men. Some were dazed and battle-struck, incapable of clear understanding. Some were as incoherent as drunkards. Some lay in an overpowering drowsiness. The most were doggedly patient and long-suffering, with a mighty longing for water obliterating every other emotion.

The Scottish Rifles' losses were four officers and 33 men killed (or died of wounds) and seven officers and 54 men wounded.

Following Black Week, Spion Kop was regarded as another humiliating setback, but the opportunity to gain a measure of revenge came a few days later at a gap in the hills which Buller believed was the key to reaching Ladysmith. To the right was a kopje called Doornkop and to the left a smaller outcrop called Vaalkrantz, which was the target given to Lyttelton's brigade. During the attack, which opened on 5 February, 2nd Scottish Rifles was in reserve with the Rifle Brigade but, according to Conan Doyle, both battalions followed 'hard on the heels' of the assault and by nightfall the whole brigade had reached the summit. However, lack of reinforcement allowed the Boers to retrench and bring up artillery, forcing 4 Brigade to retire.

By then Roberts and Kitchener had quickly taken a grip on the situation. The emphasis shifted to taking Kimberley as quickly as possible (it fell on 15 February) and in quick succession Kitchener defeated the Boers at Paardeberg and the siege of Ladysmith was lifted.

This was the turn of the tide and the war entered a new phase with the invasion of the Orange Free State and the Transvaal. By the end of the summer Pretoria and Johannesburg had been occupied and on 30 July the bulk of the Boer army under the commandant-general Martinus Prinsloo capitulated at Brandwater Basin. To all intents and purposes the war was over. The main Boer strongholds were in British possession, the lines of communication had been secured and the Boer leadership was fractured, but the fighting was destined to last another 18 months in its third and final phase. At the end of the year Roberts handed over command to Kitchener, but instead of tying up the loose ends the new commander-in-chief found himself engaged in a lengthy and bitter guerrilla war with an enemy who refused to give up the fight. During this phase of the fighting the battalion was given the task of guarding the lines of communication between Sanderton and Heidelberg, a duty which the regimental history describes as 'a monotonous and dreary existence, occasionally varied by attempts of small parties of Boers to cross the railway'. In the last stages of the war the battalion was withdrawn from 4 Brigade to take part in counter-insurgency operations against Boer guerrillas in Natal. In one operation a detachment under the command of Major Fell marched 1,268 miles without tents and only one blanket and one waterproof sheet per man. The war ended with the signing of the Treaty of Vereeniging in 31 May 1902 and 2nd Scottish Rifles returned to Glasgow two years later.

In addition to the operations carried out by the 2nd battalion mention must also be made of the contribution made by those men of the Scottish Rifles who served as Mounted Infantry in a company of Gough's Mounted Infantry under the command of Captain Ian Stewart. In common with every other regiment, the battalion provided officers and men for the Mounted Infantry, a force of 20,000 troopers who acted as scouts and rapid-response forces. The 4th Militia Battalion of the Lanarkshire Rifle Volunteers (see below) also saw service in the war, one of several formations of part-time soldiers of the militia who fought in South Africa. It was in action with 20 Brigade in the operations in Brandwater Basin at the time of the Boer surrender. Other Volunteer battalions sent reinforcements to the service companies that went to South Africa and six men served in the Scottish Cyclist Volunteer Company on communications duties.

As had happened after the Crimean War the fighting in South Africa was put under scrutiny through a Royal Commission in 1903. Most of the changes involved administration – the post of commander-in-chief was abolished – but it also led to the reorganisation of the army. A General Staff was formed to direct operations and training, plans were laid for an expeditionary force of six infantry divisions and one cavalry division, the militia was reorganised as the Special Reserve, becoming a regiment's 3rd battalion, and the Volunteers and Yeomanry were reorganised as the Territorial Force which came into being in 1908. This created a pool of part-time soldiers formed into 14 infantry divisions and 14 cavalry brigades which would be available for home defence or, with individual consent, for relieving overseas garrisons.

For The Cameronians this process entailed the reorganisation of its Volunteer Rifle battalions, which had come into being from 1859 onwards. Glasgow and the county of Lanarkshire had proved to be fertile recruiting ground for the Volunteers and the local corps had a good conceit of its abilities. Whole companies were recruited from businesses and institutions – one company was raised by the University of Glasgow – and it was a requirement for all officers to serve in the ranks before being commissioned. Some companies were made up of total abstainers; others worked together in firms such as the Etna Foundry. Another battalion, the 3rd Lanarkshire Rifle Volunteers, achieved lasting fame from the men's achievements as footballers. In December 1872 its members formed a football club which took up residence at Cathkin Park in Glasgow three years later. In the 1888–89 season the battalion won the Scottish Cup, beating Celtic in the final, which had to be replayed due to a snowstorm. Fourteen years later the links with the regiment were lost when the club became a professional entity playing under the name Third Lanark FC. The club continued playing in the Second Division until it was declared bankrupt in June 1967 and the turnstiles at Cathkin Park were closed for the last time.

It was a curiosity of the new Territorial Force order that in recognition of their beginnings as Rifle Volunteers the Cameronians' Territorial battalions tended to serve under the title 'Scottish Rifles' during the First World War (in some orders of battle there can be some confusion between the two titles, with both being used). They were organised in the following way:

5th Battalion: formed from 1st Lanarkshire Rifle Volunteer Corps, which was created in Glasgow in 1859.

6th (Lanarkshire) Battalion: formed from 16th Lanarkshire Rifle Volunteer Corps, which was created in 1873 from companies based in Hamilton, Uddington, Strathven, Bothwell, Wishaw, Motherwell and Blantyre. In 1880 it was renumbered 2nd Lanarkshire Rifle Volunteer Corps.

7th Battalion: formed from 3rd Lanarkshire Rifle Volunteer Corps, which was created in Glasgow in 1859.

8th Battalion: formed from 4th Lanarkshire Rifle Volunteer Corps, which was created in north Glasgow in 1859.

After returning to Scotland 2nd Scottish Rifles moved to Talavera Barracks in Aldershot, which was to be its home until September 1911 when it sailed to Malta, just over 100 years since the old 90th Perthshire Light Infantry had first been based on the island following the signing of the Treaty of Amiens.

SIX

The First World War: 1914–16

In the early summer of 1914 Europe witnessed a series of events that would plunge the continent into a global war. On 28 June the heir to the throne of the Austro-Hungarian empire, Archduke Franz Ferdinand, was shot dead with his wife in Sarajevo, the capital of the province of Bosnia-Herzogovina. Initially the incident seemed to be an isolated terrorist attack of a kind that was all too common in the Balkans and the first reaction was that the perpetrators would be caught and punished by the imperial authorities. Even when it was reported that the blame for the outrage was being shifted onto neighbouring Serbia, the first of the Slav states to gain independence and a source of constant irritation in Vienna, there was no reason to believe that the task of hunting down those responsible would precipitate a crisis.

However, when it became clear that neighbouring Serbia might have been implicated in the attack the crisis deepened. On 23 July, Austria-Hungary issued an ultimatum to Serbia, making ten demands for the suppression of Serb nationalist groups, the punishment of the assassins and participation in the judicial process. Serbia was given 48 hours to comply and although the response was placatory its government stopped short of allowing Austria-Hungary to take part in the trial of the assassins, arguing that the matter should be referred to the International Court at The Hague. That readiness to co-operate seemed sufficient to settle the matter but already diplomacy was proving powerless to stop Europe's drift towards war. Both countries mobilised their armed forces when Germany, Austria-Hungary's main ally, encouraged Vienna to take decisive action against the Serbs before any other country intervened in the affair. Confident of German support, Austria-Hungary declared war on Serbia five days after issuing its ultimatum, thus paving the way for a wider conflict. The following day, 29 July, Russia, Serbia's traditional friend and protector, began to deploy its forces along the border with Austria and within 24 hours this was followed by the order for full mobilisation.

Although the move was made to discourage Austria, it threatened Germany, which immediately demanded that Russia 'cease every war measure against us and Austria-Hungary'. On 1 August Germany declared war on Russia, followed two days later by a further declaration of war against France, Russia's ally. That same day German forces began crossing into Belgium as part of the pre-arranged Schlieffen Plan to bypass the heavily fortified French frontier and encircle Paris from the north through Belgium. Britain, which had wanted to remain aloof from the crisis and was not formally in alliance with any of the main participants, was now about to be pressed into the conflict through a treaty of 1839 which guaranteed Belgium's neutrality. On 4 August, no answer having been received to an ultimatum that Belgium should remain unmolested, Britain declared war on Germany.

To meet the threat Britain's armed forces put into action previously agreed plans to safeguard the country in the event of European war. At the end of its summer manoeuvres on 29 July the Royal Navy's Grand Fleet was ordered to sail from Portland through the Dover Straits north to its war station at Scapa Flow in the Orkney islands, where it was put on a war footing. The army, too, was on the move. As part of the 'Precautionary Period' of the Defence Plan Prior to Mobilisation, formations of the regular army based in Britain were told to return to their depots on 29 July. Most were on their annual summer camps or undergoing live firing exercises. The 1st battalion was at camp near Blair Atholl and one of the officers, Captain James Jack, noted in his diary that the regiment had not been in that part of Scotland since 1689 'when, under Colonel Cleland, who was killed, they defeated a large body of Highlanders at Dunkeld'. He also noted, almost by way of an after-thought, that tensions in Europe had been increasing ever since Austria declared war on Serbia. Jack, a veteran of the Boer War, had just finished playing tennis at Blair Castle when the telegram arrived ordering his battalion to return to Glasgow. On 5 August he recorded his views about the declaration of war: 'One can scarcely believe that five Great Powers – also styled "civilised" – are at war, and that the original spark causing the conflagration arose from the murder of one man and his wife . . . It is quite mad, as well as being dreadful . . .'

Across the country the battalions of the Territorial Force were also mobilised and within a few days were given the opportunity of volunteering to serve overseas instead of remaining at their depots for home defence. Most agreed, including the regiment's four Territorial battalions, whose men were drawn from a variety of backgrounds. When John Reith, later the founding father of the BBC, was commissioned in 1/5th Scottish Rifles in 1911 he observed that the 'social class of the man in the ranks was higher than that of any other regiment in Glasgow'. Whole companies had been formed from staff of Glasgow's leading business firms and one was raised from the University of Glasgow, with the result that many of the rank and file were educated members of the middle class who thought themselves equal to, if not better than, any regular formation. Amongst those who served in the battalion were two future prime ministers, Andrew Bonar Law and Sir Henry Campbell-Bannerman, and the scientist William Thomson, later Lord Kelvin. By way of contrast the 1/6th battalion drew its men from the heavy industrial towns of Lanarkshire and the 1/7th battalion had one company of total abstainers while the 1/8th battalion drew one of its companies from Glasgow's breweries.

Plans were also laid to expand the size of the army. On being appointed Secretary of State for War, Field Marshal Lord Kitchener astonished his colleagues by stating that the war would last at least three years and it would require over a million men to win it. On 8 August the call went out for the first 100,000 volunteers who would man the New Army (also known as Kitchener's Army) special service battalions. No new formations would be raised but the existing infantry regiments would expand their numbers of battalions to meet the demand for men who would serve for the duration of the hostilities. One of the New Army battalions, 13th Cameronians, was formed as a 'bantam' battalion to recruit men who were below the regulation height of 5 feet 3 inches and above 5 feet but were otherwise physically sound. The bantam concept caught on and a complete bantam division was formed, the 35th, with its distinctive rooster divisional sign, but the experiment came at a price. Many of the recruits were not only under-sized but were also physically unsound and became a liability in the front line. When the 14th Highland Light Infantry joined 40th Division at Aldershot in the spring of 1915 it had to absorb the 13th Cameronians, which had been reduced to 200 men after a series of stringent medical examinations had ruled out over 800 bantam recruits from the Glasgow area.

By the war's end The Cameronians consisted of the following

formations representing the Regular Army, the Territorial Force and the New Army:

1st Battalion (Regular Army), Glasgow, served with 19 Brigade variously in 6th Division, 27th Division, 2nd Division and 33rd Division (latterly in 98 Brigade)

2nd Battalion, Scottish Rifles (Regular Army), Malta, served in 23 Brigade 8th Division and 59 Brigade 20th Division

3rd (Reserve) Battalion (Regular Army), Hamilton

4th (Extra Reserve) Battalion (Regular Army), Hamilton

1/5th Battalion (Territorial Force), Glasgow, served with 19 Brigade variously in 6th Division, 27th Division and 33rd Division

2/5th Battalion (Territorial Force), Glasgow, served in 65th Division

3/5th Battalion (Territorial Force), Glasgow

1/6th Battalion (Territorial Force), Hamilton, served in 23 Brigade 8th Division, 154 Brigade 51st (Highland) Division and 100 Brigade 33rd Division

2/6th Battalion (Territorial Force), Hamilton, served in 65th Division

3/6th Battalion (Territorial Force), Hamilton

1/7th Battalion (Territorial Force), Glasgow, served in 156 Brigade 52nd (Lowland) Division

2/7th Battalion (Territorial Force), Glasgow, served in 65th Division

3/7th Battalion (Territorial Force), Glasgow

THE CAMERONIANS

1/8th Battalion (Territorial Force), Glasgow, served in 156 Brigade 52nd (Lowland) Division and 103 Brigade 34th Division

2/8th Battalion (Territorial Force), Glasgow, served in 65th Division

3/8th Battalion (Territorial Force), Glasgow

15th Battalion (Territorial Force), Deal, served on home defence duties

9th (Service) Battalion (New Army), Hamilton, served in 27 Brigade 9th (Scottish) Division and 43 Brigade 14th Division

10th (Service) Battalion (New Army), Hamilton, served in 46 Brigade 15th (Scottish) Division

11th (Service) Battalion (New Army), Hamilton, served in 77 Brigade 26th Division

12th (Reserve) Battalion (New Army), Nigg, served in 101 Brigade 34th Division

13th (Service) Battalion (New Army), Hamilton, served as a Bantam Battalion in 120 Brigade 40th Division after amalgamation with 14th Highland Light Infantry

14th (Labour) Battalion (New Army), Glasgow, served in France with Labour Corps

16th (Transport Workers) Battalion (New Army), Paisley

17th (Transport Workers) Battalion (New Army), Hamilton

18th (Service) Battalion (New Army), Aldershot, served in 48 Brigade 16th Division

1st Garrison Battalion (New Army), Hamilton, served in India

Creating the New Army proved to be a hit-or-miss business. Kitchener's call for the 'first hundred thousand' volunteers produced the desired numbers very quickly but the army soon found itself overwhelmed by the sheer weight of numbers. Not only did the army have to find sufficient volunteers but those men had to be trained, equipped, housed, fed and hardened for the shock of battle. At the same time the forces already in contact with the enemy on the Western Front had to be serviced and reinforced, all of which placed an immense strain on the country's economic and industrial infrastructure. It also stretched the army's capacity to the limit and to meet the need for instructors hundreds of retired soldiers were called up to instil the basic elements of drill and discipline in the rapidly expanding new regiments. At the outbreak of war Rory Baynes was home on leave from west Africa and quickly made his way to Maryhill Barracks to join the 1st battalion. Finding that he was surplus to requirements he was sent south to Bordon in Hampshire with 200 volunteers who formed the nucleus of the 9th battalion, of which Baynes became adjutant. As he found, it was a time of extreme confusion when normal standards had to make way for improvisation:

> We had absolutely nothing in the way of uniform or equipment or anything else. In spite of that we started marching quite soon, as one of the first things was to get the men as fit as possible. I think that broomsticks, instead of rifles, were the first equipment that we learnt to drill with. Then a certain amount of uniform started to arrive. This was all old full dress uniform from every kind of unit and you got a most extraordinary selection on parade. You'd see a man for instance in a rifle tunic and tartan trews, wearing a straw hat, next to somebody else in a red coat and some civilian trousers.

Following a period of rigorous training 9th Scottish Rifles crossed over to France in March 1915 and first saw action at the Battle of Festubert, in which Baynes was seriously wounded in the leg.

THE WESTERN FRONT

1st, 2nd, 1/5th, 1/6th, 9th, 10th, 11th, 13th battalions

The first Cameronians to see action were the men of the two regular battalions. Indeed, 1st Cameronians was one of the first British regiments to reach France, landing at Le Havre at 8 a.m. on 15 August when, as Captain Jack recorded, it received 'a tremendous reception, French sentries on the jetty, temporarily relaxing professional stiffness, cheer and throw their caps in the air'. Being an unattached battalion with no brigade structure the battalion was entrusted with guarding the British Expeditionary Force's (BEF) lines of communications, a task it shared with three other regular regiments, 2nd Royal Welch Fusiliers, 1st Middlesex and 2nd Argyll and Sutherland Highlanders. However, within a short time of crossing over to France from Southampton the four battalions were placed in 19 Brigade and remained under force command. This meant that the brigade commander, Major-General L. G. Drummond, reported directly to the BEF commander, Field Marshal Sir John French, and not to II Corps commander General Sir Horace Smith-Dorrien. The brigade was also tasked with providing a link to the French 84th Territorial Division as II Corps began digging into defensive positions along the Mons canal during the third week of August.

During the Battle of Le Cateau, fought on 26 August, the 1st battalion formed part of the brigade reserve for II Corps but rapidly found itself caught up in the first fierce fighting of the war. This was the British Army's biggest battle since Waterloo and it proved to be a stubborn rearguard action against overwhelming odds. Three British divisions faced the German First Army under General

Alexander von Kluck and despite defending a difficult position they were able to hold the Germans and to retire successfully towards St Quentin. During the fighting 1st Cameronians and 2nd Royal Welch Fusiliers supported 3rd Division when it was driven out of the village of Caudry in the centre of the British line. At one stage in the retreat the battalion covered 57 miles in 36 hours. Ahead lay the battles of the Marne and the Aisne, and the move into Flanders to prevent the Germans from reaching the Channel ports. This was the 'race to the sea' as the Allies plugged the gap to the north to prevent the Germans making a breakthrough on the exposed flank. As Captain A. G. Ritchie revealed in his diary for the regimental records, it was a time when men were exhausted, and it took huge reserves of commitment to stay the course:

> The men are extraordinary, far and away more disciplined and quieter and steadier under fire than they are when there is no danger. They are splendid fighting material . . . At last morning comes and another outburst of firing. I am dead tired and beginning to see things; trees suddenly leap into the air and giant men lean over me pointing huge phantom fingers at the enemy and I wake with a start in the act of falling down, terrified lest I have betrayed my trust and been to sleep. But I have only slept a fraction of a minute standing up and with my eyes open.

By then 2nd Scottish Rifles had also arrived in France. The battalion left Valletta on 15 September and arrived a week later in Southampton to join 23 Infantry Brigade together with 2nd Devonshire Regiment, 2nd West Yorkshire Regiment and 2nd Middlesex Regiment. Six weeks later the battalion crossed over to France and went into the line south-west of Messines where, according to the regimental war history, the men found 'nothing to see but bare mud walls of a narrow muddy trench, nowhere to sit but on a wet muddy ledge; no shelter of any kind against the weather except the clothes you are wearing'. For the next four winter months the situation remained the same, with the addition that the conditions were exacerbated by enemy sniper and artillery fire, both of which caused casualties. In a memoir held by the regiment, Captain M. D. Kennedy left a telling description of the hardships endured by the battalion during that first winter of war on the Western Front:

> No one who was not there can fully appreciate the excruciating agonies and misery through which the men had to go in those days before anti-'trench-feet' measures were taken, and other similar methods adopted, to make trench life more endurable. Paddling about by day, sometimes with water above the knees; standing at night, hour after hour on sentry duty, while the drenched boots, puttees and breeches became stiff like cardboard with ice from the freezing cold air. Rain, snow, sleet, wind, mud and general discomfort all added their bit to the misery of trench life.

The first battle, Neuve Chapelle, was initiated by Sir John French to win back a German salient captured in October 1914. This position gave the Germans the freedom to fire on British positions from both flanks and the danger had to be eliminated, but French hoped to exploit any success by threatening the German lines of communication between La Bassée and Lille. The British field marshal was also anxious to demonstrate to his doubting French allies that his forces had retained their offensive capability and had a significant role to play in the war. By then the British military presence in France and Flanders had expanded and the attack would be made by formations of the British First Army under the direction of General Sir Douglas Haig – IV Corps, consisting

96th (CAMERONIAN) REGIMENT, 1864.

R. Simkin

Although raised as a Scottish regiment the 26th Cameronians did not wear tartan until 1881 when it was amalgamated with the 90th Perthshire Light Infantry. As this painting of 1864 by Richard Simkin shows, the men dressed as a typical British line infantry regiment.

(Courtesy of South Lanarkshire Council)

In the middle of the nineteenth century the 90th Perthshire Light Infantry saw service with the Light Division during the Crimean War. A group of officers relaxing – then as now dogs were popular companions.

(Courtesy of South Lanarkshire Council)

In the all-male world of the officers mess its members were encouraged to participate in off-duty sporting activities. Polo and shooting were popular pastimes in The Cameronians, but as this late Victorian cartoon shows, there were other ways of letting off steam. (Courtesy of South Lanarkshire Council)

Warrant Officers and sergeants of the 11ᵗʰ battalion in 1915 before leaving for Salonika. During the First World War The Cameronians raised 27 battalions for service on the Western Front, Gallipoli, Palestine and Salonika. (Courtesy of South Lanarkshire Council)

Two of the Territorial battalions, 7th and 8th, served with 52nd (Lowland) Division in the ill-fated Gallipoli campaign. In 1916 they moved to Egypt to serve in the campaign against Ottoman forces in Palestine. (Courtesy of South Lanarkshire Council)

Three thirsty Cameronians relax over a glass of beer in the late 1950s. After the Second World War the regiment was reduced to one Regular battalion and one Territorial battalion. RQMS Spiers, centre, enlisted in 1933 and left the army in 1961. (Courtesy of South Lanarkshire Council)

In 1966–67 the regiment completed a highly successful tour of duty in Aden in which it was involved in internal security duties during a period of heightened tensions within the colony. The only obvious bonus was the sunshine. (Courtesy of South Lanarkshire Council)

In May 1968 The Cameronians held its disbandment parade at Douglas in Lanarkshire, close to the spot where the regiment was founded in 1689. The 1st battalion marched onto the parade ground under the command of its commanding officer Lieutenant-Colonel Leslie Dow.

(Courtesy of South Lanarkshire Council)

of 7th Division, 8th Division and the Lahore Division and Meerut Division of the Indian Corps. The plan was to attack on a narrow front of only 2,000 yards using four infantry brigades in the initial assault phase. Amongst those taking part was 2nd Scottish Rifles, which had been deployed to attack on the right flank of 23 Brigade with 2nd Middlesex on the left.

When the attack began at 7.30 a.m. on 10 March it achieved complete surprise. The huge British bombardment also encouraged the waiting infantrymen to believe that no one could have survived the shelling and when they began their attack half an hour later hopes were high that an early breakthrough could be achieved. Subsequent war histories and contemporary documents refer to the British and Indian infantry sweeping through the German lines unopposed and creating a huge breach which opened up the prospect of a quick local victory by advancing a mile into German-held territory. Unfortunately that was not the case in the 23 Brigade attack. Both the Middlesex and the Scottish Rifles found the enemy barbed wire intact and their lead companies came under heavy and sustained German machine-gun fire when they reached the uncut German barbed wire. Following the example of Captain E. B. 'Uncle' Ferrers, commanding B Company, most of the officers in 2nd Scottish Rifles carried their swords into battle but that chivalric style was no armour against the rattle of machine-gun fire and the Scottish riflemen were 'forced to fall back and lie in the fire-swept open'. The monocled Ferrers was wounded, sword in hand, and within an hour the battalion had lost most of its officers and sergeants, killed or wounded.

As the battalion regrouped, a fresh artillery bombardment on the German positions finally silenced the enemy fire but by mid-morning 23 Brigade was unable to continue the attack and the 2nd Scottish Rifles took up a defensive position to the north of Neuve Chapelle. There was further fighting the following day and on 12 March there was a renewed attack to try to break out of Neuve

Chapelle, but by then the battle was already slipping out of the hands of the British commanders. Communications between the front lines and rear areas broke down quickly and decisively. There was no radio or telephone link and messages had to be sent by runners, with the result that the assault formations were unable to make contact with headquarters. For the battalion commanders this proved to be fatal as orders were painfully slow to get to the front lines or did not arrive at all, so that there was a complete breakdown in command and control. Initially taken by surprise, the Germans responded with a will and rushed reinforcements into the line and were soon in a position to counter-attack. However, those assaults failed to make any headway due to the fact that the British forces had also been able to regroup their defensive lines, and when the battle was finally called off that same evening the losses on both sides were high – the British lost 11,652 casualties killed, wounded or taken prisoner and the Germans an estimated 8,500. When 2nd Scottish Rifles was relieved on the night of 14/15 March the battalion consisted of 143 men under the command of a young officer, 2nd Lieutenant W. F. Somervail, and Regimental Sergeant-Major Chalmers. The battalion had lost 13 officers and 112 other ranks killed and 344 were either lost or wounded. Amongst them was its commanding officer, Lieutenant-Colonel W. M. Bliss, whose arrival a year earlier had caused consternation because he was 'a 1st battalion man'.

The next major fighting of 1915 was the ambitious Allied plan to attack the German line from the Hohenzollern Redoubt to the town of Loos while the French attacked to the south at Vimy and in Champagne. Ahead of the main assault, which began on 25 September, gas was used in addition to a huge artillery bombardment and in the early stages hopes were high of achieving a breakthrough. Both the 9th and 10th battalions succeeded in reaching their objectives – respectively Hill 70 and part of the

Hohenzollern Redoubt – but it came at a cost. During the first wave of the assault made by 46 Brigade, 10th Scottish Rifles lost 21 officers and 464 other ranks killed, wounded or missing. The 2nd battalion also took part in the battle, although it was not involved in the first phase, being held in reserve for a subsidiary move to the south undertaken by 8th Division. By then James Jack was serving with them as commander of B company, having spent time in England on sick leave, and he was not disappointed by what he found on his return: 'All ranks here, some 700, of the 90th Light Infantry, the old "Perthshire Grey Breeks"... are in fine fettle. What else could they be with such a Commanding Officer [Lieutenant-Colonel G. T. Carter-Campbell]? I do not believe that a better battalion landed in France.'

Alas, for all the great hopes, Loos was not a success; indeed it has been labelled as an unnecessary battle which caused high casualties for no perceivable gains. At the end of the month the French attack in Champagne was brought to a standstill, and coupled with the failure at Vimy the Allied autumn offensive achieved little in return for huge losses. Bowing to the demands of the French, Haig kept the battle going in the British sector until 16 October, by which time the British casualties at Loos and the subsidiary attacks amounted to 2,466 officers and 59,247 other ranks, killed, wounded or missing. Heavy losses in the 1/5th and 1/6th battalions forced them to amalgamate on 29 May 1916 and to serve as 5/6th Scottish Rifles.

For that battalion and other Cameronian battalions serving on the Western Front (1st, 2nd, 9th and 10th) the major event of 1916 was the Battle of the Somme, which began on 1 July and ended at the end of November. During the battle the regiment's Regular, Territorial and New Army battalions took part in the following main actions:

THE CAMERONIANS

1–8 July: Montauban and Bernafay Wood (9th battalion)

1–2 July: Ovillers (2nd battalion)

14 July: Longueval (9th battalion)

15–18 July: Bazentin Ridge (1st and 5/6th battalions)

20 July–31 August: High Wood (1st and 5/6th battalions)

15 September: Martinpuich (10th battalion)

October: Butte de Warlencourt (9th and 10th battalions)

October: Transloy (2nd battalion)

23 October–13 November: Transloy (1st and 5/6th battalions)

First in action on 3 July was the 9th battalion, which attacked on the right of the line against German positions at Bernafay Wood. Fighting alongside 6th King's Own Scottish Borderers the battalion began the attack from Montauban only to find that the wood, though occupied, was undefended. However, hostile bombardments continued and the eventual casualties in the battalion were 32 killed, five died of wounds, 100 wounded and two missing. Worse followed in the middle of the month when 9th (Scottish) Division attacked German positions in the area west of Longueval on the edge of Delville Wood. When the assault was called off on 18 July the 9th battalion had been reduced to 335 effectives and was withdrawn from the Somme front to recover and regroup.

During that same period 2nd Scottish Rifles was in brigade reserve on the La Boiselle Salient where James Jack noted that 'our lads are in grand form, quite carefree, itching to cross the parapet to meet the Hun and sure of victory'. Even so, casualties were sustained when 23 Brigade came under enemy fire and the battalion lost one officer and one other rank killed and five officers and 60 other ranks wounded. Two weeks into the battle the 1st battalion took over the line near High Wood and immediately suffered casualties from intensive German artillery fire. East of Bazentin-le-Petit 5/6th Scottish Rifles suffered a similar fate, losing five men killed and three officers and 76 other ranks wounded in a 48-hour period. At the beginning of August 15th (Scottish) Division arrived from the Loos Salient and took over the trenches at Martinpuich. Once again the main problem was the weight and intensity of the German shelling. In one attack on 14 September 10th Scottish Rifles lost all the officers of B Company, leaving Company Sergeant-Major Baxenden in command. Later he was commissioned and awarded the Military Cross. The following day there was a measure of revenge when the battalion attacked the German lines under a heavy barrage which, according to the regimental history, gave the enemy no inkling of what was happening:

> Caught as they were about to have breakfast, the attack was
> a complete surprise. This was fortuitous. The men of the
> 10th battalion quickly consumed the steaming hot coffee
> which greeted their arrival and helped themselves liberally
> to a quantity of cigars which they found.

During the raid the battalion captured over 300 prisoners for the loss of 41 killed and 250 wounded.

The final phases of the battle were marked by continuous rain which not only made operations difficult but turned much of the area into a quagmire. When the weather improved, as it did in the second week of October, it allowed the 9th battalion to be involved in the attempts to take the Butte de Warlencourt, a position which would provide the British with better observation of the German lines. The site of a prehistoric burial ground, it dominated the surrounding countryside but, as 9th Scottish Rifles found, its mass of tunnels and trench systems made it a formidable obstacle and it was not captured until the following year. As the divisional history made clear, the weather had played havoc with the German defensive systems guarding the position:

> There seemed to be absolutely no bottom to the communication trenches and the men struggled along waist-deep in mud. Darkness had fallen when they reached the trenches near Eaucourt l'Abbaye and an intense hostile barrage added to the horror. With devilish accuracy the shells pitched near the communication trenches and many plunged right into them. Unspeakable was the fate of any man who was badly wounded that night; he sank below the mire and the men in the rear pressed on, all unconscious that the welcome firmness, which momentarily sustained them, was the body of a comrade . . .

So deeply entrenched in the national consciousness is the Battle of the Somme that it has become a byword for all that appeared to be wrong-headed in the tactics employed on the Western Front. Its trenches and its battlefields gave it historical substance, the mud of Flanders represented the awfulness of its conditions in winter and everywhere firmly etched place names recalled the great battles of attrition where thousands of soldiers were killed in what have come to be represented as senseless death-dealing attacks. As an arena of combat the Western Front certainly does not lack critics. In his memoirs written after the war David Lloyd George, prime minister from 1916, excoriated the 'policy of flinging masses of our troops against concrete machine-gun emplacements, with the result that hundreds of thousands of them were put out of action' and another politician involved in the direction of the war, Winston Churchill, a future prime minister, later admitted that while he said nothing at the time he viewed 'with the utmost pain the terrible slaughter of our troops and the delusions that were rife' during the Battle of the Somme. Even the normally phlegmatic and unemotional James Jack felt compelled to confide to his diary that he was in 'poor spirits' for most of the time – he was second-in-command of 2nd Scottish Rifles during the battle – and the loss of friends had badly shaken his faith:

> 'Except ye *believe in* (not *serve*) Me, ye shall in no wise enter My Kingdom' – a harsh threat, I thought, that no gentleman would utter to any servitor who, not in this world of his own accord, nevertheless carried out his duties to the best of his ability, maybe giving his life for them.
>
> Well, I laughed, if this is to be the reward of Service, however lacking the Faith, many will have scored over Providence by giving All, free, gratis and for little or nothing, for the honour, perhaps, of a grave on a battlefield.

On 27 August Jack was ordered to take over command of 2nd West Yorkshire Regiment and 'walked along a few hundred yards of trench in the Hohenzollern Support Line to take over my new duties'. Many soldiers felt the same way that Jack did and the fighting on the Somme seems to have bred a sense of fatalism allied to a belief (which Jack also shared) that the job had to be done and that the enemy had to be defeated. Covenanting stoicism there was aplenty within all the battalions but humour, too, was never far, the soldier's stock response to keep bad luck at bay. The recently discovered diaries of Captain Alexander Stewart, an older Cameronian officer, reveal a not untypical picture of the soldier's response to higher authority:

> I am very much annoyed by memos sent round from Headquarters that come in at all hours of the day and night; they stop me getting a full night's rest and some of them are very silly and quite unnecessary. When I am very tired and just getting off to sleep with cold feet, in comes an orderly with a chit asking how many pairs of socks my

> company had a week ago; I reply 141 and a half. I then go
> to sleep; back comes a memo: 'please explain at once how
> you come to be deficient of one sock'. I reply 'man lost his
> leg'. That's how we make the Huns sit up.

The entry is dated 9 November 1916. By then the fighting on the Somme had almost come to an end and the Allies had lost 600,000 casualties, two-thirds of them British, while the German losses cannot have been much less.

GALLIPOLI

1/7th, 1/8th battalions

The stalemate on the Western Front encouraged thoughts of opening a second front and the opportunity was provided by Turkey's entry into the war in December 1914. The target was Constantinople, capital of the Ottoman Empire, which could be attacked through the Dardanelles to allow a joint British and French fleet to enter the Black Sea following the destruction of the Turkish forts on the Gallipoli peninsula. At that point it would have been safe to land ground forces to complete the capture of the peninsula and to neutralise the Turkish garrison. However, the plan was stymied by the sinking of several Allied capital ships and a consequent loss of nerve in the high command. Following the failure of the naval operations to destroy the Turkish forts it was decided to land troops at Cape Helles on 25 April but the landings were opposed by the Turks, who offered stout resistance. By the end of the month the British had suffered around 9,000 casualties, one-third the size of the attacking force in return for little ground gained. Reinforcements were required and amongst them were 1/7th and 1/8th Scottish Rifles as part of 156 Brigade in 52nd (Lowland) Division, which began landing in the peninsula in the first week of June. The other battalions in the brigade were 1/4th and 1/7th Royal Scots.

THE FIRST WORLD WAR: 1914–16

After spending some time in the trenches to acclimatise and become used to the enervating operational conditions on the peninsula, 156 Brigade first saw battle on 28 June, when it attacked a Turkish position at Helles known as Fir Tree Spur. The attack was a fiasco as the British artillery had failed to suppress the enemy's machine-gun positions and the four battalions paid a heavy price. Although both the Royal Scots battalions fought their way through to the Turks' second line, 1/8th Scottish Rifles ran into heavy fire and within five minutes had lost over 400 casualties killed or wounded. Amongst those killed was the commanding officer, Lieutenant-Colonel H. M. Hannan. Acting as brigade reserve, the 1/7th battalion reinforced the assault but it fared no better, losing 14 officers and 258 casualties. So great were the losses in both battalions that they had to be merged and served for the remainder of the campaign as 7/8th Scottish Rifles and were unable to resume their separate identities until February 1916. Some idea of the conditions facing the battalion can be found in the regimental history which contains a graphic description of the aftermath of the attack at Helles:

> The wounded lay where they had fallen in the saps and in No Man's land without succour, suffering from thirst and maddened by flies. It was not possible to rescue those who lay out between the opposing lines until nightfall. There they remained with a broiling sun like burning brass high overhead. The tragedy is that morning culminated in the sun-scorched grass and scrub of No Man's Land bursting into a devouring flame. Many helpless wounded perished.

Despite the arrival of reinforcements – in all, the British commander General Sir Ian Hamilton was given five new divisions – the deadlock could not be broken and the men on the peninsula were becoming increasingly weakened. An ambitious amphibious landing at Suvla Bay failed in August because the Turks were able to rush reinforcements into the area to prevent the creation of a bridgehead. In October the inevitable happened: Hamilton was sacked, rightly so as his leadership had become increasingly feeble and sterile, and he was replaced by General Sir Charles Monro, a veteran of the fighting on the Western Front. Having taken stock of the situation he recommended evacuation, although this was not accepted until the beginning of November when Kitchener himself visited the battle-front and found himself agreeing that the difficulties were insuperable. In a brilliant operation, which was all the more inspired considering the fiascos which preceded it, the British finally withdrew their forces at the end of 1915, remarkably without losing any casualties. The great adventure to win the war by other means was finally over.

As happened on other fronts during the war the exact British death toll was difficult to compute but most estimates agree that 36,000 deaths from combat and disease is not an unreasonable tally. The official British statistics show 117,549 casualties – 28,200 killed, 78,095 wounded, 11,254 missing. Total Allied casualties were put at 265,000. Most of the survivors were sent back to France in time to take part in the Battle of the Somme while others, including the 52nd (Lowland) Division, were sent to Egypt to guard the Suez Canal and to train for the forthcoming operations against Ottoman forces in Palestine and Syria.

SEVEN

The First World War: 1917–19

Arguments still rage about the Battle of the Somme and the effect that it had on the Allied war effort. The disastrous opening day saw the greatest level of losses ever suffered by the British Army, the final death toll shows that over one million soldiers were lost by all sides and the offensive only allowed the Allies to move their line forward by seven miles. Yet, it was not all disaster. In the cold statistical analysis of modern warfare the Allies had done better than the Germans out of the fighting on the Somme and with the benefit of hindsight it can be claimed as 'a win on points'. While the expected breakthrough never occurred and the ground gained was an extremely modest return for the expenditure of so many lives, pressure had been taken off the French in the southern sectors and valuable lessons had been learned. After the war senior German commanders admitted that the Somme was 'the muddy grave of the German field army' while their opposite numbers in the British Army argued that the inexperienced New Army divisions had come of age during the battle, even though most of the lessons were bloodily learned.

The battle had also forced the enemy to re-appraise their options. Rightly fearing the renewal of a bigger Allied offensive in the same sector in the new year the German high command decided to shorten the line between Arras and the Aisne by constructing new and heavily fortified defences which would be their new 'final' position behind the Somme battlefield. Known to the Germans as the Siegfried Stellung and to the Allies as the Hindenburg Line, this formidable construction shortened the front by some 30 miles and created an obstacle which would not be taken until the end of the war. The withdrawal began on 16 March and as the Germans retired they laid waste to the countryside, leaving a devastated landscape in which the cautiously pursuing Allies had to build new trench systems. To meet this new challenge the Allies planned a fresh spring assault on the shoulders of the Somme Salient with the French attacking in the south at Chemin des Dames while the British and Canadians would mount a supporting offensive at Arras and Vimy Ridge. Prior to the British attack which began on 9 April there would be a huge and violent bombardment with 2,879 guns firing 2,687,000 shells over a five-day period.

THE WESTERN FRONT
1st, 2nd, 5/6th, 9th, 10th, 11th, 13th battalions

On the opening day of the battle 9th Scottish Rifles attacked with 27 Brigade along the line between Point du Jour and Athies, and succeeded in reaching its first line objectives, as did 10th Scottish Rifles in the attack to the south on Monchy Le Preux. Both battalions attacked in a biting wind which sent snow flurries scudding across the countryside, but despite the wintry weather the portents were good. For the first time the assault battalions found that the artillery had done its job by destroying the wire and new types of gas shells had fallen in the rear areas, killing German transport horses and making the movement of guns impossible.

Within a few hours the German line had been penetrated to a depth of two miles and in one of the most astonishing feats of the war the Canadian divisions swept on to take the previously impregnable German positions on the gaunt features of Vimy Ridge. The first day of the assault was a triumph for the British and the Canadians, who suffered reasonably small casualties and succeeded in taking their first objectives and then regrouping to attack the second and third lines of defence. Casualties in the 9th battalion were two officers killed and 65 rank and file killed and wounded in return for an advance over one and a half miles. In the same period the 10th battalion lost two officers killed and two wounded and 20 rank and file killed and 112 wounded.

Three days later the 10th battalion was relieved and returned to regroup in Arras. That same day, 12 April, 9th Scottish Rifles was ordered to take the village of Roeux and the chemical works which lay 1,000 yards to the north of the Scarpe River between Fampoux and Plouvain. This produced some of the fiercest fighting of the battle, with the village changing hands several times. In the opening rounds of the attack the battalions reached the chemical works only to find that it had not been touched by the artillery barrage. Worse, the Germans enjoyed an open field of fire and the attacking British infantrymen made tempting and easily identified targets as they advanced across the snow-covered ground. As the regimental history put it, the Scots 'offered a target which must have astonished and elated the defence'. The battalion's casualties were correspondingly high: five officers wounded or missing, 34 rank and file killed and 136 wounded.

While this drama was unfolding both the 1st and 5/6th battalions attacked on the right of the British Third Army between Croisilles and the River Scarpe. During the attack of the 1st Cameronians it came under heavy machine-gun fire and was quickly pinned down; 5/6th Scottish Rifles fared little better and lost four officers killed and five wounded and 39 rank and file killed and 155 wounded. Among the casualties was Sergeant John Erskine, who had been awarded the Victoria Cross in the previous year (see Appendix). On 15 April, almost a week after the first attack, Haig succumbed to reason and to the pleas of his divisional commanders and called a halt to the opening rounds of the battle to allow reinforcements to be brought up. In the next phase, which opened on 23 April, 10th Scottish Rifles attacked east of Guemappe and in one engagement succeeded in capturing 60 Germans and three machine guns. A fortnight later 9th Scottish Rifles was involved in 9th (Scottish) Division's attack on a position known as Greenland Hill, which was heavily defended and resulted in periods of hand-to-hand fighting in the German trench systems. The battalion's casualties were two officers killed and six wounded and 12 rank and file killed and 174 wounded. Both the 1st and 5/6th battalions resumed their assault on the Hindenburg Line on 15 May but during a week of continuous fighting 1st Cameronians had been reduced to 13 officers and 350 rank and file. So depleted was 19 Brigade that 5/6th Scottish Rifles had to attach 100 of its men to 2nd Royal Welch Fusiliers.

The next major battle of 1917 was the Third Battle of Ypres, also known as Passchendaele, which was fought to deepen the British-held Ypres Salient. The battle opened in July, lasted four months and accounted for a quarter of a million casualties, 70,000 of them killed or drowned in the lagoons of mud which covered the battlefield. In the opening rounds on 31 July, 2nd Scottish Rifles attacked on the Bellewaarde Ridge but came under heavy German fire from a position known as Clapham Junction, where the attack faltered. During the operation the battalion lost three officers killed and eight wounded and 35 rank and file killed and 138 wounded. On the left 10th Scottish Rifles attacked under a creeping barrage towards the Ypres–Rouler railway line and succeeded in reaching its objectives. However, the onset of heavy rain held up progress and, as the regimental history explained, this change of weather was to have a deleterious effect on the battlefield:

> At dusk rain was falling steadily, and within a short time the ground, pitted with shell-holes, became a sea of mud and water. In peacetime the land possessed a good drainage system, but now the intricate network of surface and subsoil drains, patiently designed and executed by the industrious Belgian agriculturalists, were destroyed by shelling. The numerous streams which started in the small valleys on the ridge ran across the line of the advance, and at their lower courses, being obstructed by the shell-fire, had become sloughs. Even in good weather the water table was generally near the surface and, as the soil was clay or sand or a mixture of both, the steady downpour of rain transformed the shallow valleys into sheets of sticky mud and water. The bombardments and barrages made muddy shell-craters, the mud everywhere being the consistency of cream cheese. Guns and tanks sank. Men sank. To this was added the horror that men once wounded might drown in the water or suffocate in the mud.

By the middle of August the ridge had still not been taken. Further operations saw 2nd Scottish Rifles in action at Hanebeek while the 10th battalion attacked Gallipoli Farm and the 9th battalion attacked the Zonnebeke Redoubt. Despite the appalling conditions operations resumed on 26 October and the battle officially came to an end on 10 November 1917. The year ended with the Battle of Cambrai, when tanks were first used in large numbers to smash through the German lines. This time the expected breakthrough occurred, with tanks penetrating the German lines to a depth of five miles within the first ten hours, but the action was not exploited and 1917 ended in frustration for the Allies on the Western Front.

In an all-or-nothing attempt to regain the initiative to win the war before US forces entered it the Germans planned a major offensive for March 1918. This would drive a wedge between the two opposing armies, striking through the old Somme battlefield between Arras and La Fère before turning to destroy the British Third and Fifth armies on the left of the Allied line. Codenamed 'Michael', it opened with a massive rolling 'hurricane' artillery barrage followed by a rapid and aggressive advance by the infantry designed to punch a hole in the British defences and lay the foundations for defeating the enemy in Flanders. Strong-points would be bypassed to be wrapped up later by the mopping-up troops. The fighting began in the early hours of the morning of 21 March when the German artillery produced a huge bombardment which lasted for five hours and which left the defenders badly shaken and disoriented. Gas and smoke shells added to the confusion, which was increased by an early morning mist, leaving commanders with no exact idea of where and when the infantry attack was coming. Fog on the battlefield did not help matters and the experience of 9th Scottish Rifles while defending the Crozat Canal gives a good indication of the confusion which was caused by the unexpected German attack:

> Screened by fog which lingered over the low ground, the enemy crept up to the railway embankment unseen from the right as well as the left, and twice small parties crossed over and threw grenades. Sharp fighting ensued, with nothing but the embankment between. Finally, about 11 a.m., when the fog lifted, a continuous stream of Germans could be seen pouring round the left some five hundred yards to the north-west, and the position on the embankment became untenable. There was no option but to withdraw.

During the operation and the subsequent withdrawal the battalion lost three officers killed and four wounded and 35 rank and file killed and 140 wounded. Over 150 were listed as missing and many of these were found later to have been killed in action. Assessing the actual number of deaths is difficult. Regimental war diaries tabulated the casualties after the battle but the number listed as 'killed' invariably increased in the aftermath as men died of their wounds and those listed as 'missing' were found to be dead. For example, the War Diary of the 10th Scottish Rifles listed 239 missing, but of those 192 were later found to be dead and the adjutant admitted the impossibility of verifying the actual numbers. At one point in the early days of the German assault 2nd Scottish Rifles was reduced to 64 effectives, but despite heavy losses across the whole of the British front there was no decisive German blow.

The Michael offensive was finally called off on 5 April without the strategically vital town of Amiens coming under threat of attack. The German break-in battle had succeeded in capturing a large salient but it proved difficult to hold and the attempt to break through and split the Allies had failed to materialise. There had also been heavy German casualties – some quarter of a million killed, missing or wounded – and morale within the assault formations had been shattered by their failure to produce a decisive blow in the so-called 'Kaiserschlacht' (Kaiser's Battle) which was supposed to win the war. Four days later, on 9 April, General Erich von Ludendorff launched Operation Georgette, a second attack aimed along a narrow front south of Armentières in the Ypres sector. An under-strength Portuguese division was brushed aside in the Aubers–Neuve Chapelle sector, allowing the Germans to advance towards the defensive line of the rivers Lawe and Lys which was eventually shored up by the British XI Corps. During this third phase of the fighting the 1st and 5/6th battalions were involved in the successful defence of the line at Meteren while the 9th battalion was part of the defence of the vital position of Mont Kemmel. To meet a shortfall in manpower there was a radical internal reorganisation of the brigade structure, with each brigade being reduced to three infantry battalions. As a result 9th Scottish Rifles was transferred to 43 Brigade in the 14th (Light) Division in which it served for the remainder of the war.

The stand on the River Lys took the sting out of the German attack and although the enemy advanced beyond Merville and Bailleul to come within sight of Hazebrouck the arrival of French reinforcements from General Maistre's 10th Army on 21 April stabilised the front. A week later Ludendorff called off the Georgette operation, bringing a degree of respite to the battered British First and Second armies, which had taken the brunt of the attack in the Ypres sector. By then the Territorial battalions in 52nd (Lowland) Division had arrived back in France following their deployment in Gallipoli and the Middle East. After retraining to accustom them to the type of fighting on the Western Front, together with the remaining Cameronian battalions, they were part of the army which eventually defeated the Germans later in the year. As part of the reorganisation of the field army 1/8th Scottish Rifles moved to 103 Brigade in 34th Division in which it ended the war. One of the last battalions in France was 18th Scottish Rifles, which was formed mainly from the disbanded 6/7th Scottish Rifles. Following the Armistice in November both the 8th and 9th battalions marched into Germany as part of the army of occupation.

After 1,564 days of fighting the arrival of peace created a mixture of emotions – relief that the guns were finally silent and elation amongst the survivors but, inevitably perhaps, the high spirits were tempered by the memory of lost loved ones and by the sobering thought that the jubilation masked much sadness in many homes.

In a letter written to his father on 5 October 1917, Lieutenant James Burnett Lawson, 2nd Scottish Rifles, had argued that the best was still to come and that the fighting spirit in his battalion was as high as it had ever been:

> No wonder there are wars. No wonder Haig's men have to smash their way up the Passchendaele heights. He is taking the inevitable road to victory. That's why there must be no faltering. Give way to nerves now, and all our suffering will have been in vain. Let us rather steel our hearts for the second half of the great fight which begins next Spring and ends with complete victory in October 1918.

Lawson was one month out in his calculations but he did not live to see the 'complete victory' which he forecast with such enthusiasm. A medical student from Glasgow, he had enlisted in The Cameronians in 1915 and was killed in action leading a counter-attack at Meharicourt during the Germans' spring offensive. For his parents the tragedy was compounded when they learned that their son had sent in his papers to be allowed to return to his medical studies under a scheme introduced by the government early in 1918. During the fighting on four fronts – France and Flanders, Gallipoli, Palestine and Salonika – the regiment's losses were 7,106 killed and over 11,000 wounded. After the war, on 9 August 1924, the regiment unveiled its own memorial in the grounds of Kelvingrove Park in Glasgow. Designed by Philip Lindsey Clark, the memorial shows an infantryman surging forward between a machine-gunner and a wounded comrade. The determination on his face is perhaps at odds with the notion of remembrance, but it is a thoroughly realistic and unsettling depiction of the reality of warfare.

EGYPT AND PALESTINE

1/7th, 1/8th battalions

Following the end of the Gallipoli campaign 1/7th and 1/8th Scottish Rifles were based in Egypt with 52nd (Lowland) Division prior to the opening of a new front against the forces of the Ottoman Empire in Palestine. The operation was entrusted to an Egyptian expeditionary force of 88,000 soldiers under the command of General Sir Edmund Allenby, who had been sacked after his failure at Arras in April 1917. Before taking up his new command he had been warned by Lloyd George that he had to take Jerusalem by Christmas as a gift to the British nation and that he should demand what he needed to make sure the enterprise succeeded. In fact there was already a pressing need to attack the Turkish forces, which were being reinforced in Aleppo in present-day Syria for an offensive to retake Baghdad. If Allenby could engage the enemy through Palestine it would force the Turks to divide their forces and pass the initiative back to the British.

From the outset Allenby recognised that he needed overwhelming superiority over the Turks if he were to avoid the setbacks at Gallipoli and Mesopotamia, but getting the reinforcements in the second half of 1917 was another matter. The priority continued to be the Western Front and with the Battle of Passchendaele eating up resources it took time and much subtle diplomacy for him to build up his forces. Eventually these consisted of a Desert Mounted Corps made up of Anzac and British cavalry and yeomanry regiments and two infantry corps, one of which contained the 52nd (Lowland) Division which had been moved to Egypt following the withdrawal from Gallipoli. Their objective was to break into Palestine through Gaza and Beersheba and destroy the defending Turkish Eighth Army. On arrival in Egypt all battalions were re-equipped and dressed in new khaki cotton drill tunics and shorts and began training in desert conditions. For the men of the two battalions – re-formed in Egypt with drafts from home – there was also the opportunity to learn how to deal with the camels which were used instead of wheeled transport. Each beast had its own camel-driver but even so, as the war history records, new skills had to be learned:

> A camel carried a load of about 350 lb, which must be well and properly balanced otherwise it will fall off or be shaken off deliberately. The load is put into rope nets and fastened on to both sides of a wooden saddle. These balanced loads are made up beforehand in readiness for the driver, who will cause the camel to lie down so that they can be roped to the saddle, one on each side. It was soon discovered that the Arab driver would 'barrak' the animal (i.e. make it lie down) but he would not load it. Therefore the troops had to do the loading themselves. It took them over two hours on that first day. Later on in the campaign, after much practice, they were able to load a battalion's entire camel transport ready to move off in six minutes.

The two battalions' first operational service took place at Romani, on the eastern side of the defences for the Suez Canal. In August the Turks made a determined advance on the British lines but were driven off at Wellington Ridge south of the town. The next phase saw the Allied forces move across the Sinai Desert towards El Arish and Rafa, where the Turks' defensive line was centred on Gaza. The first fighting took place in April and May but the British failed to dislodge the Turkish positions in Gaza and lost over 6,000 casualties in so doing, most of them suffered by the 52nd (Lowland) Division; the losses in the two Scottish Rifle battalions were three officers and 32 rank and file killed and nine officers and 168 rank and file wounded. However, the Scots got their revenge in the third battle, which opened on 31 October and ended on 7 November when the Turks were forced to retire. Following good work by the Australian cavalry the decisive strike was made at Sheria, where the enemy was quickly outflanked and forced to retire. During this mobile phase of the battle the Turks fought with great determination but they were demoralised by the weight of the attack and by the use of British warplanes to strafe their fleeing columns. The casualties suffered by the two battalions in the Third Battle of Gaza were four officers killed and eight wounded and 68 other ranks killed and 222 wounded. During the battle all the battalions in the division endured nine days of continuous fighting and marched a total of 69 miles, mainly in pursuit of the retreating Turkish forces.

To great acclaim Jerusalem fell on 8 December after a determined attack by the 53rd and 60th divisions forced the remaining defenders to evacuate their positions. Three days later, in a carefully stage-managed operation, Allenby and his staff entered the city to take possession of it and to secure the holy places. It was not the end of the war in Palestine, but it was the beginning of the end. Allenby's next objectives were to move into Judea and to regroup to prevent Turkish counter-attacks before moving on to his next objectives, Beirut, Damascus and Aleppo. However, to accomplish that he would need additional troops to reinforce his own men and to protect the lines of communication as he pushed north; at the very least, he told the War Office, he would need an additional 16 divisions, including one of cavalry. In the short term his forces invested Jaffa, which fell after the 52nd (Lowland) Division seized the banks of the River Auja in an operation which demanded surprise and, according to the divisional War Diary, resulted in 'the most furious hand-to-hand encounters of the campaign'. The passage of the Auja proved to be one of the most difficult operations of the campaign in Palestine. Coracles were used to ferry many of the men across; it took considerable skill to construct pontoon bridges linked by rafts and there were considerable delays in creating the necessary bridgeheads. And once on the other side the men had to advance across an unknown landscape in the dark. A diary kept by Lieutenant-Colonel J. M. Findlay commanding 1/8th Scottish Rifles gives an idea of the difficulties encountered by his men as they went into the attack with 1/7th Royal Scots against Turkish positions south of Muannis:

> As soon as we turned east through the lower orange groves we encountered difficulties. The groves were fairly thick and the men fell into the drains which were dug between every second row of trees. There they stuck and had to be rescued. However, we continued our stealthy movement ... Our small advanced guard came to a Turkish (battalion) Headquarter's House which they surrounded and after some bombing and some vehement adjurations in Turkish (learned for the occasion), succeeded in capturing the place, taking prisoner three officers, including a battalion commander and sixteen other ranks besides an amount of war materiel, a number of machine guns and two Arab stallions, one of which I annexed and rode regularly for the next two or three months ...

To commemorate the feat three marble columns were removed from the old crusader castle at nearby Arsuf and placed on the spots where the three brigades had crossed the Auja. This proved to be the last action undertaken by the majority of the Scottish regiments in Palestine. Before the question of reinforcing Allenby could be addressed by the War Office the Allies were faced by the crisis on the Western Front in March 1918. The need for rapid reinforcement came at the very moment when Allenby wanted to continue the push towards Aleppo and he was forced to order two infantry divisions, nine yeomanry regiments and one divisional artillery unit to move to France in March 1918. One of the divisions was 52nd (Lowland), which embarked for Marseilles at Alexandria aboard seven troopships escorted by six Japanese destroyers.

SALONIKA

11th battalion

The withdrawal from Gallipoli allowed the British and the French to build up forces in the Balkans, both to support Serbia and to prevent Bulgarian forces from influencing events in the region – on 5 October 1915 its army had been mobilised and it entered the war on the side of the Central Powers. The Allied response was to send two divisions to the port of Salonika (now Thessaloniki) under the command of the French General Maurice Sarrail. At the time German and Austro-Hungarian forces commanded by Field Marshal August von Mackensen had invaded Serbia and had entered Belgrade while Bulgarian forces had pushed into Macedonia, a move which stymied any Allied attempt to relieve pressure on the Serbs. As a result Sarrail's divisions were pushed back into Salonika, which rapidly became a huge military base. By the end of the year three French and five British divisions, together with a huge amount of stores and ammunition, were encamped in a perimeter which the Germans ridiculed as 'the greatest internment camp in the world'. Amongst them was 11th Scottish Rifles, a New Army battalion which served in 77 Infantry Brigade with 8th Royal Scots Fusiliers, 10th Black Watch and 12th Argyll and Sutherland Highlanders.

The main action in Salonika took place in May 1917 with an operation by the French and Serb forces to break through the Bulgarian defensive lines. The British objectives were the heavily defended positions to the west of Lake Doiran but the Allied offensive failed and had to be abandoned on 23 May with the loss of 5,024 British casualties. As happened on the Western Front, the Allied artillery failed to cut the wire and the attacking infantry soon found themselves pinned down by accurate Bulgarian artillery and machine-gun fire. An entry in the 11th battalion's War Diary for 8 May indicates the extent of this problem:

> The various Coys [companies] had reached their respective objectives but had been cut up and repulsed. A great deal of confusion was also occasioned by the dust and smoke caused by the bombardment. The enemy's bombardment in No Man's Land excellent.

Other problems came from manpower shortages, lack of reliable equipment, especially heavy artillery, and the absence of coherent plans. In the initial stages of the assault 8th Royal Scots Fusiliers had been held in reserve but as the attacks by the other three battalions began foundering it was then used to reinforce them in the later phases of the fighting. Heavy and accurate Bulgarian artillery fire forced the British forces to call off the attack and for the rest of the year the front remained surprisingly quiet while XVI Corps' activities in the Struma valley were confined to minor operations which did not warrant the distinction of being described as battles.

During the winter Greece finally entered the war on the Allied side following the abdication of the pro-German King Constantine and at last the Allies were rewarded for their long-standing military presence in Salonika. Weakened by German troop withdrawals the Bulgarian army failed to halt the last assault of the war, which began on 15 September and ended a fortnight later when the Bulgarian front was split. Known as the Second Battle of Doiran, the Allies launched 200,000 in the attack on the much-weakened enemy lines, with the British leading the flank attack and the Greeks on Strumitsa to the east. In the opening stages 77 Brigade moved forward to take its assigned positions but heavy enfilading machine-gun fire forced a withdrawal to regroup. The War Diary of the 11th battalion recorded tersely what happened next: 'Seeing this Corporal Fisken of N. 1 Coy dashed forward with his Lewis gun and put the enemy machine-gun out of action. After very sharp fighting the second objective was taken.'

At one point the battalion was reduced to throwing rocks at the enemy due to an acute shortage of ammunition. By then the brigade isolated and the smoke and dust created by the artillery fire prevented them from giving or receiving messages from divisional headquarters. Men were becoming increasingly exhausted; in the chaos, and expecting a Bulgarian counter-attack, Brigadier-General W. A. Blake took the decision to retire and abandon the position, with the battalions being ordered to make good their escape as best they could carrying their wounded and their equipment. Both the Scots Fusiliers and the Scottish Rifles managed to pull out, but in the mayhem of the noise of battle and the thick clouds of smoke and dust, 12th Argylls stumbled into a Bulgarian position and lost 50 per cent of its fighting strength, a significant percentage of the 7,103 British casualties killed and wounded. The losses in 11th Scottish Rifles were three officers killed or died of wounds and 12 wounded and 173 other ranks killed or missing. It was the last significant battle of the campaign. On 29 September French forces entered Skopje and the following day Bulgaria requested an armistice. Their new commander General Franchet D'esperey was keen to continue his advance up through the Balkans to threaten Germany's southern flank and his troops were already crossing the Danube when the war came to an end on 11 November. At the same time British forces moved up to the Turkish frontier but any hopes of attacking Turkey ended when the Turks signed an armistice on 31 October. Elements of British forces remained in the area into 1919, serving as peacekeepers, and for most of them it was a dispiriting end to a campaign which had tied up huge numbers of men and materiel for no obvious strategic gains. Although the British Salonika Force listed a modest 18,000 casualties from combat, this was overshadowed by the 481,000 who had succumbed to illness, mainly malaria.

Following the Armistice 11th Scottish Rifles was part of a force which was taken to guard the Romanian border at Ruschuk south of Bucharest. It also spent time occupying the port of Dobruja on the Black Sea until April 1919, when it was sent to Egypt to carry out internal security duties. It remained in that country until December, when it was finally disbanded; it was the last of the Cameronian New Army battalions to be stood down at the end of the First World War.

EIGHT

The Second World War: 1939–43

As had happened throughout Britain's history, the conclusion of hostilities brought an immediate reduction in the huge wartime armed forces. All New Army battalions were disbanded and there were substantial reductions in the size of the Territorial Army. For The Cameronians this meant that the 5th and 8th battalions were amalgamated as 5/8th Cameronians (Scottish Rifles) while the 6th and 7th battalions retained their separate identities. For the two regular battalions the post-war years brought their own share of excitements, with deployments in China, Egypt, India, Iraq, Kurdistan and Palestine. Both battalions also spent periods at home stations and in most respects it was a case of 'business as usual' as they went back to the familiar patterns and routines of peacetime soldiering. Following the construction of the huge volunteer and conscript army, the post-war Regular Army returned to its position as an all-volunteer force and horizons narrowed as regiments went back to a way of life that all professional soldiers recognised and understood. A bottleneck in promotion prospects also led to complacency and to a comatose condition which discouraged radical thinking and put a stop to reform. Pacifism, arising largely from the huge death toll from the war, was also a disincentive for change. All too often anti-war sentiments became anti-armed forces sentiments and the army suffered as a result.

In June 1919 the 1st battalion re-formed at the Curragh in Ireland largely from men drawn from the 3rd (Special Reserve) Battalion. It remained in the country until November 1922, when it moved to Aldershot. In January 1927 it was mobilised for service in China under the command of Lieutenant-Colonel E. B. Ferrers, a survivor of the 2nd battalion's action at Neuve Chapelle 12 years earlier. A shortage of soldiers meant that numbers had to be made up with men from 17 other regiments. Following a 43-week deployment in Shanghai and Kowloon the battalion returned to Catterick, then to Glasgow, before moving to Egypt in January 1930 for a tour of duty which lasted until October 1931. Its next station was Lucknow in India, where it was involved mainly on internal security duties. India was destined to be the battalion's home for the rest of the decade, with moves to Landi Kotal on the North-West Frontier in 1936 and Barrackpore in Bengal in 1937. A highlight of the battalion's life in India was its skill at polo and boxing, in which sports it won several tournaments. It also continued to add to the regiment's reputation in small-arms shooting competitions.

During the same period 2nd Scottish Rifles had a succession of more variegated experiences. It re-formed at Colchester in April 1919 prior to a deployment in India, where it commenced training in mountain warfare at Kohat and Tirah on the frequently troublesome North-West Frontier. As part of the gradual Indianisation of the Indian Army, Indian officers were being granted the king's commission and as a result Iskander Ali Mirza, the first Indian officer to pass out of Sandhurst, served with the battalion at Kohat. Later he reached the rank of major-general and later still, between 1956 and 1958, he served as President of Pakistan. (Another out of the ordinary Cameronian officer was Qaboos bin Said al Said, later Sultan of Oman, who served with the 1ˢᵗ battalion in Germany in the early 1960s.) In February 1923, following a rebellion by Kurds in Iraq, which had become a British mandated territory as a result of the Treaty of Versailles, the battalion embarked for Basra and joined a brigade-sized column which moved north towards Erbil. Overall command of the operations was in the hands of the Royal Air Force, which was using a new policy of Air Control or 'aerial policing' to dominate the country and provide internal security. This involved aircraft to attack or discourage disaffected areas, but the tactics also demanded the use of ground forces, hence the deployment of 2ⁿᵈ Scottish Rifles. During the operations, which lasted from 2 March to 15 May, the battalion marched 475 miles over harsh terrain and usually in unforgiving temperatures.

On returning to India the battalion was based at Quetta and Nowshera before returning to Glasgow at the end of 1929. When it arrived at Maryhill Barracks the 1ˢᵗ battalion was about to depart for Egypt; it was the first time that the two battalions had been together in Scotland since the regiment had formed in 1881. In October 1933 the battalion moved south to Bordon in Hampshire under the command of Lieutenant-Colonel Rory Baynes, and three years later it proceeded to Palestine at a time of heightened tension between Arabs and Zionist settlers. As happens so often in this kind of insurgency war, the duties were difficult and extremely demanding, with intensive patrolling and the ever-present danger of terrorist attack. As the regimental history explained, the whole Arab population was officially engaged in a strike and this 'meant that a large proportion of the younger Arabs had nothing better to do than make mischief, and in consequence ambushes and other outrages had increased'. At the end of the year the battalion returned to Bordon before moving north to Catterick in Yorkshire. By then the political situation in Europe was deteriorating.

In Germany the Nazis had come to power under Adolf Hitler and their presumptuous territorial claims were soon trying the patience of the rest of Europe. In 1938 Prime Minister Neville Chamberlain seemed to have bought 'peace in our time' following his negotiations with Hitler in Munich, which gave the Germans a free hand in the Sudetenland and subsequently in Bohemia and Moravia. However, it proved to be the calm before the storm. Having signed a peace pact with the Soviet Union, Hitler then felt free to invade Poland at the beginning of September 1939. Chamberlain, who would be replaced as prime minister by Winston Churchill the following year, had no option but to declare war – Britain and Poland were bound by treaty – but the country's armed forces were hardly in a fit condition to fight a modern war. The British Army could put together only four divisions as an expeditionary force for Europe, six infantry and one armoured division in the Middle East, a field division and a brigade in India, two brigades in Malaya and a modest scattering of imperial garrisons elsewhere. Years of neglect and tolerance of old-fashioned equipment meant that the army was ill-prepared to meet the modern German forces in battle and British industry was not geared up to make good those deficiencies. Once again in the nation's history it seemed that Britain was going to war with the equipment and mentality of previous conflicts. Events in Poland quickly showed that Germany was a ruthless and powerful enemy whose *Blitzkrieg* (lightning war) tactics allowed them to brush aside lesser opposition: using armour and air power the Germans swept into the country, which fell within 18 days of the invasion, allowing Hitler to turn his attention to defeating France.

To meet the challenge the British government made belated attempts to strengthen the armed forces and this entailed a rapid expansion of the Territorial Army. This also meant that one battalion had to give up its infantry roles: in 1938 5/8th Cameronians was given an anti-aircraft role, becoming 56th Searchlight Regiment

Royal Artillery. The regiment's other battalions, 6th and 7th, and their duplicates, 9th and 10th, all served as infantry while a 12th battalion served in the home defence role as did the 11th, 13th and 30th battalions, which were not field force units but were composed mainly of middle-aged men. Throughout the Second World War the Territorial battalions appeared on orders of battle as Cameronians (Scottish Rifles), a result of the slackening of differences between the 1st and 2nd battalion during the 1930s. In keeping with that new regimental feeling the 2nd battalion was now generally referred to as 2nd Cameronians (Scottish Rifles).

FRANCE

2nd, 6th and 7th battalions

At the outbreak of hostilities the 2nd battalion was part of 5th Division, in which it served in 13 Infantry Brigade with 2nd Royal Inniskilling Fusiliers and 2nd Wiltshire Regiment. As had happened in the First World War, the British government went to the immediate assistance of its French allies by dispatching a new British Expeditionary Force under the command of Field Marshal Lord Gort. Composed of two corps of two infantry divisions each, plus supporting arms, and eventually numbering 152,000 men, it began moving across to France in September. Amongst the first to arrive was the 2nd battalion, which arrived in Cherbourg on 12 September and moved towards Comines on the French–Belgian border. The ground force was accompanied by 12 RAF squadrons but it had no armoured division and few tanks. Later in the year it was strengthened by another infantry division and in 1940 it was further reinforced by eight Territorial divisions including the 51st (Highland) Division, which was sent into the line on the Saar front. Most of these formations were inadequately trained and poorly equipped, but by the summer of 1940 the BEF numbered 394,165 men, the majority in defensive positions.

During this period, which came to be known as the 'phoney war', the 2nd battalion was involved in building defensive positions on the Ypres–Comines canal and the War Diary recorded that life consisted mainly of digging trenches and training for battle. All that changed in the spring. First the Germans invaded Norway in April and then on 10 May they launched an attack in strength towards Holland and Belgium. By way of response the British moved their forces forward into Belgium and for the 2nd battalion at least the war history records that the move was well received:

> The Battalion was greeted by the Belgians with the greatest enthusiasm. Cheering crowds lined the roads and bread, cigarettes, etc., were freely distributed. As yet there were no thoughts of withdrawal and the streams of refugees moving West, which were encountered later, had not commenced.

On 17 May 2nd Cameronians had its first experience of battle when it was attacked by German aircraft near Lemberg and claimed its first 'kill' when D Company shot down one of the enemy raiders. Then came the orders to begin withdrawing as the British and their French allies proved unable to halt the rapid tide of German military aggression. Lens was reached on 21 May and it soon became clear that the British position was becoming untenable. Hopes were pinned on a counter-offensive, as had happened in September 1914, but the available forces were depleted in strength – the battalion was reduced to a headquarter company and two rifle companies – and information was scant. On 28 May the battalion received orders to withdraw from Wytschaete and to make its way with the rump of the BEF to the Channel coast at Dunkirk. During the final embarkation the battalion contrived to keep its heavy weapons and returned almost intact to England. During the operations 2nd Cameronians lost 360 casualties killed and wounded.

In May, in a last-ditch attempt to shore up the French, the government deployed a number of divisions in Normandy, including 52nd (Lowland) Division which arrived on 13 June, but they were quickly withdrawn when the position became hopeless. Together with the other battalions in the division, 6th and 7th Cameronians did not take part in any of the fighting during the Battle for France. 'It had been a fine gesture and a gallant effort to support the French Armies to the last,' wrote the regiment's war historian but, as he also admitted, the grim reality of warfare insisted that the reinforcements be withdrawn 'if we were to survive as a nation'.

INDIA AND BURMA

1st battalion

Following the outbreak of war in Europe 1st Cameronians was based in Secunderabad but it was soon needed for active service operations when Japan entered the war in December 1941. The reason for the deployment was the fall of Burma to a rapid and successful Japanese assault in the aftermath of the infamous pre-emptive air strike on the US Pacific Fleet's base at Pearl Harbor in Hawaii on 7 December 1941. This was followed in quick succession by further Japanese attacks on the islands of Guam, Wake and Midway while the Japanese Second Fleet escorted General Tomoyoku Yamashita's Twenty-Fifth Army to attack the north-west coast of the Malay peninsula. The fall of Hong Kong on Christmas Day 1941, and the later fall of Singapore on 15 February 1942, were followed by the collapse of British power in the Far East and the threat that India itself might fall into Japanese hands. Equally disastrous was the retreat from Burma which followed its invasion by the Japanese from Raheng in Thailand. Originally the Japanese had not been interested in occupying the whole country and believed that their strategic needs would be served by taking the port of Rangoon and the airfields on the Kra isthmus but their minds were changed by the realisation that Britain could use Burma as a springboard to attempt to retake Malaya and also by the threatening presence of the Chinese 5th and 6th Armies to the north along the lines of communication known as the Burma Road.

The Japanese plan to rectify the situation was based on a three-pronged attack – on Rangoon, the Salween river and the Sittang river – and as had happened in Malaya they relied on speed and aggression to accomplish their objectives. In the last week of February the 1st battalion's initial deployment was to Pegu, some 45 miles north of Rangoon, a vital railway junction and bridgehead where the line was being defended by 17th Indian Division under the command of Major-General J. G. Smyth VC. On 11 February the Japanese had crossed the Salween, the retreating 17th Indian Division blew the bridges across the Sittang three days later and by 18 March Rangoon had fallen. It was a time of chaos and confusion and the battalion did not receive a direct role until 23 February, when it became the support group for 7 Armoured Brigade, and for the rest of the month its tasks were largely confined to patrolling the area and assisting stragglers. All the while the Japanese were probing the British defences and making inroads as they simply bypassed British positions – a tactic which had worked well in the invasion of Malaya. On 7 March Pegu was abandoned and the battalion carried out a succession of withdrawals towards Prome, which was reached at the end of the month. As the situation deteriorated the new defensive position proved to be only a stopping place as the battalion continued its retreat towards the Irrawaddy.

Although the British and Indian forces counter-attacked in the Irrawaddy Valley until the beginning of May, they were outflanked to the east and to the west where the Japanese drove General Chiang Kai-shek's army back towards the Chinese border. Short of supplies, exhausted and demoralised, the two armies went their separate ways and the British and Indian forces began what came to be known as 'the longest retreat in British military history'. Following a march of 900 miles the survivors crossed over the border into India on 19 May: of the original 30,000, 4,000 were dead and another 9,000 were missing. Despite the setback – no soldier likes to retreat – 1st Cameronians had acquitted itself well in the close-quarter fighting against the Japanese and had certainly not been overawed by an enemy which quickly came to be thought unbeatable. By the time the battalion returned to India it numbered little more than a company, many of the casualties having fallen victim to malaria, but as the commanding officer, Lieutenant-Colonel W. B. Thomas, recorded, regimental pride was still intact:

> The campaign in Burma in 1942 was a defeat, but one from which we learned many lessons. Possibly the chief one was that with determined troops the Jap could be, and was, fought to a standstill; also that in a number of engagements he had been defeated by troops who were very tired and often short of food and ammunition.
>
> In the Battalion we soon sifted the wheat from the chaff. It was a campaign in which we made many friends, and we all had the greatest confidence in our commanders. Perhaps never in the long history of the Regiment has the discipline been higher, and it was founded on comradeship and the principle of share and share alike.

In July 1942 the Japanese high command made plans for 'Operation 21', a three-pronged attack from Burma towards Ledo, Imphal and Chittagong. It was over-ambitious as the terrain in northern Burma was not suited to the type of rapid offensive operations used so successfully in the Malay peninsula, but the fact that India was threatened was enough to convince British minds that their position was precarious. At the same time, Indian nationalists were making increasingly strident demands for Britain to quit India and there was a clear and immediate need to restore British prestige by taking the offensive back to the Japanese and retrieving lost ground in Burma. The first of these initiatives was the first Arakan campaign, which opened in September 1942 and which was aimed at capturing the Akyab peninsula following an advance from Chittagong by way of Cox's Bazaar and Donbaik. However, by the following May the Japanese had retrieved all the ground won during the advance; for the British it was not only an expensive failure which cost over 5,000 casualties but it inculcated a belief that the Japanese were unbeatable jungle fighters.

It was against that background that the first steps were taken to retrieve the position. For the first time, specially trained British and Indian soldiers showed that they were capable of taking on and beating Japanese soldiers in the fastnesses of the Burmese jungle. The creator of the turnaround was Major-General Orde Wingate, a remarkable gunner officer with unorthodox opinions, who had served in Palestine before the war and had earlier helped the Emperor Haile Selassie to return to his throne in Ethiopia. He believed that the Japanese could be overcome by inserting long-range penetration forces which would operate behind enemy lines and destroy vital objectives. Fighting in eight columns supplied from the air, the force was called the Chindits, after the Burmese word 'chinthe', the mythical winged beasts which guarded Buddhist temples, and it went into action in February 1943. Operation Longcloth (as it was known) was a partial success. It sowed confusion in the minds of the Japanese high command, who feared it was a precursor to a large attack and tied up troops to hunt down the Chindits. The Mandalay–Myitkyina railway line was cut, but the cost was appalling. Of the 3,000 men who carried out the operation, only 2,182 came back; around 450 had been killed in action and the remainder were either lost or had been taken prisoner. Only 600 of the force were able to return to soldiering. Nevertheless, Wingate had shown that the Japanese could be fought on their own terms and the Chindits were a huge propaganda success, so much so that a second, larger, operation was planned for the spring of 1944. When planning started for Operation Thursday, as it would be known, 1st Cameronians was assigned to the new force and so entered into an association with a general with whom the regiment had much in common. Not only did Wingate have a Scottish ancestry (the family came from Glasgow and Stirlingshire), but, by coincidence, as a child he had worn a kilt of Douglas tartan.

MADAGASCAR

2nd battalion

On returning from Dunkirk the survivors of the 2nd battalion assembled at Huntly in Aberdeenshire, where it received fresh drafts of reinforcements and replacement weapons. Its immediate task was coastal defence duties in Banffshire and Morayshire, but at the end of the month it moved south to Crieff before moving again to Liverpool, its home until March 1941. Northern Ireland was to be its next station and it remained in County Armagh until the spring of 1942, when it received orders for an overseas posting. With the rest of 5th Division, 2nd Cameronians left for India in a convoy which sailed the long route around Africa to reach its destination. When it arrived in Durban orders were received for 13 and 17 Brigades to join a new force which had been raised to take part in the invasion of the French colony of Madagascar off the east African coast. Initially, the governor of the island had thrown in his lot with the Free French forces under the command of General Charles de Gaulle but he changed his mind and resigned his post after the destruction of the French fleet by the Royal Navy at Mers-el-Kebir (an operation ordered by Churchill to prevent the

French warships being used by the Germans). He was replaced by a representative of the Vichy government, General Armand Léon Annet. That altered the strategic balance in the region, as the Vichy government collaborated with the Germans, and in March 1942 the British received intelligence that Germany had persuaded Japan to occupy the island as a means of gaining naval superiority in the Indian Ocean, a move that would threaten strategic supply routes. To prevent that happening a British invasion force, Force 121, was put together under the command of Major-General Robert Sturges, consisting of 17 and 29 Brigades and No. 5 Commando, with 13 Brigade as a strategic reserve. In the first major amphibious operation of the conflict and the first ambitious landings since Gallipoli in 1915, Sturges' primary task was to capture the northern naval base at Diego Suarez with support from a naval task force under the command of Rear-Admiral Neville Syfret.

With air cover provided by strike aircraft of the Fleet Air Arm flying from the carriers *Indomitable* and *Illustrious*, the first assault was made against Diego Suarez on 5 May. Although Operation Ironclad achieved complete surprise, the resistance was surprisingly strong and the fighting for the port and the town of Antsirane (now Antseranana) lasted for three days before the French capitulated. However, it was not the end of the struggle, as the French governor retreated to the south of the island with the rump of his forces. On 6 May 2nd Cameronians finally came ashore and played a role in the final mopping-up operations.

PERSIA AND SYRIA

2nd battalion

Although the battalion had been part of the reserve in Madagascar and had not seen much action, it had been given invaluable experience of operating in tropical conditions and this was to stand it in good stead for the next role undertaken by the division.

Having re-embarked the ground forces the convoy arrived in Bombay on 29 May and 2nd Cameronians was then taken by rail to Ahmednagar. Shortly after arriving it received orders to proceed to Persia (later Iran), where it formed 'Paiforce', a mixed force of British, Indian and Polish troops which had been formed under the command of General Sir Henry 'Jumbo' Maitland Wilson to guard the strategically important oil fields in the Persian Gulf. At the time Germany had attacked the Soviet Union and its armies had pushed deep into Russian territory as far as the Caucasus. British intelligence decrypts of top secret German Enigma signals confirmed that an enemy attack on the Middle East through the Balkans was a key part of Hitler's future plans. If the Soviet Union succumbed quickly – as was thought possible – the Germans would then be able to turn their attentions to the Middle East, using Trans-Caucasia as a jumping-off point.

Hitler also hoped that an Allied collapse would encourage the Arab peoples to rise against the British in the Levant, Palestine, Transjordan (later Jordan), Iraq and Egypt, thus tying down valuable Allied forces to deal with revolt and public disorder. It also raised the fear that the Germans would push further south and threaten Britain's interests in the Persian Gulf. If those fell, the route to India would be at risk and that would inevitably damage Britain's capacity to continue fighting the war. As a result British, Polish and Indian forces were rushed to Persia and 2nd Cameronians landed at Basra in Iraq at the end of August, the height of the hot season. From there it moved by rail to Kermanshah before taking up residence at Qum, south of Tehran. This was to be its home until the beginning of 1943, when the Red Army's crushing defeat of the Germans at Stalingrad removed the threat to Persia.

From Persia the battalion made its way westwards, first by rail to Baghdad and then by motorised transport across the desert to Dera in Transjordan. Its final destination was Kaft Coq on the slopes of Mount Hernon in Syria where it began training in mountain warfare. At the start of the war Syria had come under the control of the Vichy French administration, the collaborationist regime under Marshal Pétain formed after the defeat of France in 1940, but a year later the Allies successfully invaded the country to prevent it being used as a base for German military aircraft. Later in the summer 2nd Cameronians moved to Tripoli in Lebanon, where the first four-wheel-drive vehicles were delivered and instruction was given on the new PIAT shoulder-fired weapon (Projector, Infantry, Anti-Tank), which proved to be effective against most types of German tanks. While these experiences were interesting in themselves, and the battalion did not lack for training, it was a trying time, as the war history makes clear:

> From the time of leaving Glasgow in March 1942 . . . the 2nd Cameronians had been almost continually on the move. They had moved by almost every type of transport, experienced climate varying from intense tropical heat to extreme cold and trained in practically every kind of warfare. It had been a disappointment to all ranks not to be actively engaged against the enemy, but this was soon to be remedied . . .

At long last, on 10 June the battalion was moved to a sealed camp at El Shatt in Egypt where the men found that their next destination would be Sicily. After a peripatetic existence which had earned the 5th Division the nickname of the 'Cook's Tour Mob', it was finally going into action in earnest.

SICILY AND ITALY

2nd battalion

Following the successful outcome of the Battle of El Alamein in October 1942, where the Eighth Army commanded by General

Bernard Law Montgomery had defeated the German Afrika Korps, British and US forces were able to attack Sicily as precursor to the invasion of Italy. The operation called for a British invasion by Montgomery's Eighth Army between Syracuse and the Pachino peninsula on the island's south-eastern coast, while the US I and II Armored Corps under the command of Lieutenant-General George S. Patton would land on a 40-mile front along the southern coast between Gela and Scoglitti and Licata on the left flank. There would also be an airborne assault carried out by the US 82nd Airborne Division and the British 1st Airborne Division to attack targets in the inland area and to secure the landing grounds. Once ashore Montgomery planned to create a bridgehead and secure the ports of Syracuse and Licata before moving rapidly north to take Messina while Patton's forces covered the left flank.

On 10 July the first elements of 5th Division went ashore south-west of Syracuse, the plan being for two brigades to secure the beach-head and to allow 13 Brigade to pass through it and push inland. This was achieved successfully and a number of Italian prisoners were taken but before the brigade concentration area could be secured 2nd Cameronians had to take the small town of Floridia which dominated the high ground on the north–south road. This was duly accomplished, with the battalion losing 13 casualties killed and wounded. From there the division made its way north to Augusta, where the road was littered with the detritus of war – crashed aircraft, burning vehicles and dead bodies. From there the battalion moved with the rest of the division into the Plain of Catania, which was described in the war history in the following terms:

> A flat, naked depression, stretching for some twelve miles to
> the north, bounded on the right, or eastern, side by the sea,
> with the port of Catania in the North-East corner. From

Catania westwards ran the foothills of Etna to the high ground above Gerbini and Sferro, some fifteen miles inland to the West. The plain was principally divided by the river Simeto and its southern tributary, the Dittaino, which both ran in the plain from West to East. From south to north the main coastal road went to Catania as did the railway, running almost parallel, but a mile or so further inland. Several secondary lines and roads served the few houses, farm buildings and signal boxes that were infrequent dots in this vast expanse.

It was unpromising territory but it had to be secured if the advance were to maintain its timetable. Unfortunately, it was also a countryside which was made for defence. Towering over the plain was the smoking bulk of Mount Etna, which the enemy used to good effect to observe the Allied movements. The Germans also enjoyed air superiority and although some airfields had been captured by the Allies it took time for aircraft to arrive and to mount sorties against the enemy. Topographical considerations prevented Montgomery from utilising his superiority in armour and artillery and the lack of a decent road system meant that the infantry had to return to foot-slogging. The presence of civilians in the battlefield areas was also a hindrance. In short, after the freedom of movement enjoyed in North Africa the Eighth Army found itself hemmed in and the Plain of Catania proved to be a difficult hurdle. On the night of 13–14 July an airborne operation by 1 Parachute Brigade failed to take the vital bridges at Primasole and as a result Catania remained in enemy hands.

During this phase of the advance the battalion was able to act with armoured support from the County of London Yeomanry, although use was also made of aggressive infantry patrols. In one action on 2 August a fighting patrol led by Lieutenant J. M. Porter destroyed two German machine-gun positions and took ten Germans prisoner, including an officer. Porter was awarded the Military Cross and Corporal R. Smith the Military Medal. The next objective was the River Simeto, which had to be crossed to allow the battalion to attack the town of Paterno, which fell on 6 August. By then the end of the campaign was in sight. Sicily fell ten days later but some of the gloss was taken off the victory when over 100,000 German and Italian soldiers were evacuated across the Straits of Messina to fight again in Italy. However, the battle for the island showed that British and US forces could work in tandem against a determined enemy. Before the culmination of the campaign the battalion was taken out of the line south of Paterno to refit and to begin training with 5th Division for the next stage of the campaign in Italy. Fresh clothes were issued, equipment was cleaned and restored and the warm summer weather raised spirits. The men were also much heartened when Montgomery visited the battalion on 26 August to deliver a pep talk and to thank them for their participation in 'a model campaign'.

Having driven the Germans out of North Africa and secured Sicily, the Allies followed up their successes with the invasion of Italy in September 1943. At the same time the Italians decided to surrender, and while the Allies dithered over acceptance of the terms the Germans moved 16 divisions into Italy to continue the war and these forces were to prove more than a handful to the Allies. The Allied plan was to use the US Fifth Army to land south of Salerno and to seize Naples while the British Eighth Army, led by XIII Corps (5th Division and 1st Canadian Division), would make its assault across the Straits of Messina to secure Calabria and the extreme south of peninsular Italy. The 2nd battalion was in the first assault phase, crossing by landing craft in the afternoon of 3 September and landing unopposed at Catona. Meeting little resistance they pushed up through Calabria towards Potenza to link up with the US Fifth Army and British X Corps which had landed at Salerno and immediately encountered determined German resistance. At the end of the first week the 5th Division had moved 100 miles and by 16 September had reached the Gulf of Policastro where XIII Corps was tasked with guarding the US Fifth Army's right flank. During this phase of the operation 13 Brigade, including 2nd Cameronians, was re-embarked and taken by sea to a new position south of Gioia. It was at this stage (8 September) that the Italians surrendered, although the 2nd battalion did not notice any difference as 'it merely regularised the non-participation of the Italian soldiers in the fighting – an event which had already taken place'. On the other hand, it also encouraged the Germans to fight with greater determination, and that stubbornness was to be a feature of the fighting in the months to come.

Another move by sea took the battalion further north, to Sapri, on 16 September – the Eighth Army was determined to make as much ground as possible in the south before the German reinforcements arrived from the north. In one month, September, 2nd Cameronians advanced a total of 260 miles either by marching or by sea and only very occasionally by motorised transport. Opposition, too, was sparse and for most of October 13 Brigade acted as flank guard on the south and south-west of the Eighth Army. By then the weather conditions were deteriorating and the Allied armies were moving into more difficult territory as they advanced slowly north. From the account in the regimental war history it is clear that the Allied planners now faced a predicament: they had achieved much since landing in southern Italy but the arrival of German reinforcements had stiffened resistance along the Gustav Line which ran from the River Sangro on the Adriatic to the estuary of the River Garigliano on the Tyrrhenian Sea, 40 miles north of Naples:

A very substantial part of the country was, therefore, under Allied control and it was important that this success be exploited as soon as possible. There were many factors which made it unlikely that a straightforward drive up the leg of Italy would lead to quick or spectacular results. The Germans had been reinforced and had by now deployed and reorganised their forces. The country was almost ideal for defence, weather conditions were bad and likely to remain so for some weeks.

Faced by a position which amounted to stalemate, the Allies decided to regroup before planning a US amphibious landing to the north at Anzio (see Chapter Nine), which would give them the opportunity of attacking Rome by bypassing the Gustav Line. At the same time 5th Division was taken out of the line prior to moving into the Fifth Army and 2nd Cameronians ended the year at Castiglione, where it had been ordered to guard the rear of the Divisional Headquarters. There was a moment of sadness when Lieutenant-Colonel Eric Brickman left the battalion having served with it continuously from 1939 as a company commander, second-in-command and latterly as commanding officer. He was succeeded by Lieutenant-Colonel A. M. Finlaison, a Cameronian officer who had been commanding 2nd Wiltshire Regiment. The year ended with heavy falls of snow which blocked supply routes and made any movement so difficult that the battalion's rations had to be dropped by aircraft.

NINE

The Second World War: 1944–45

From the outset of US involvement in the Second World War the Chiefs of Staff in Washington adopted a 'Germany First' policy. Although the shock of the Japanese attack at Pearl Harbor suggested that the defeat of Japan should be given priority, the strategic balance in 1942 slipped away from the Allies. The Philippines fell into Japanese hands in May, by which time the Dutch East Indies had also been attacked and occupied; command of the sea had also been lost and all that remained to the Allies was the Hawaii naval base, the garrison on Midway Island and the US carrier fleet which had been at sea during the Japanese attack. In fact, the need to deal with Nazi Germany had been discussed by US strategists as early as 1938 and was underscored at the first summit meeting between US President Franklin D. Roosevelt and Winston Churchill in Washington in December 1941 when the two leaders agreed that Germany would have to be defeated before they turned their attention to Japan. The conference also led to the establishment of the Combined Chiefs of Staff, composed of the British Chiefs of Staff and the American Joint Chiefs of Staff. Its first task was to begin the timetable for the invasion of Europe and to lay plans for a direct attack on Germany by invading France and driving quickly into Germany.

The opening of this second front would also take pressure off the Soviet Union, which had been invaded by German forces in the summer of 1941 and was fighting for its survival. To meet that need General George C. Marshall put forward plans for a cross-Channel invasion as early as autumn 1942 but it would only take place if Germany appeared to be weakening or if the Soviet Union needed a diversionary attack to prevent an imminent collapse on the Eastern Front. Otherwise, the invasion would take place the following spring. Marshall was bullish about both plans and believed that by attacking the heart of Germany the war would be shortened. Unless that happened, he argued, the Soviet Union would collapse and the war against Germany would last for a further decade and would require the creation of 200 divisions to win it. However, Churchill opposed the idea and argued forcefully for a US invasion of North Africa. The clash between the rival plans put the coalition under immediate strain. Marshall thought that the North African campaign was a sideshow which would do nothing to dent the German war effort; only a direct attack on the German homeland would bring the war to an end. On the US side there were also fears that the British plan was aimed at propping up its imperial holdings – the Mediterranean and the Suez Canal was the traditional route to India and the Far East. The stalemate was broken by Roosevelt, who postponed the plans in the summer of 1942 to give priority to the defeat of the Axis forces in North Africa and Sicily followed by the invasion of Italy.

A year later, in May 1943, the decision was taken to press ahead with the invasion of north-west Europe and planning for it began under joint US–British direction immediately after the Washington summit had ended. The main desiderata for the cross-Channel amphibious attack were quickly established: a landing area with shallow beaches and without obstacles which was within range of Allied air power, the neutralisation of local defences to allow a build-up which would equal the strength of the German defenders and the presence of large ports for reinforcement and re-supply. Deception also formed part of the plan: the idea was to persuade the Germans that the assault would be made across the narrowest part of the English Channel at Pas de Calais where the beaches were shallow and led into the hinterland without the obstacles of cliffs and high ground. It also offered the opportunity to make a quick strike into the Low Countries and from there into Germany. All those reasons made Pas de Calais the ideal place for invasion, but because it was the obvious location it was quickly discounted as the Allied planners knew that their German counterparts would deploy the bulk of their defensive forces there. By the end of the summer the plan was shown to the Allied leadership at the Quadrant conference in Quebec. The chosen landing ground was the Baie de la Seine in Normandy between Le Havre and the Cotentin peninsula, an area which met all the criteria, including a deepwater port at Cherbourg.

The initial planning called for an invasion force of three divisions plus airborne forces which would create a bridgehead through which reinforcements could be landed quickly to break out into Normandy and Brittany. Success would depend on the ability of the Allies to build up forces more rapidly than the Germans, and with that in mind it would be essential to deny the enemy the chance to reinforce the landing grounds by destroying road and rail communications in northern France. Although Montgomery agreed with the main principles of the plan, he put forward an alternative proposal to attack in greater weight along a broader front and with a larger airborne contribution. It was agreed that the initial assault should be made by five divisions, two US, two British and one Canadian, with one British and two US airborne divisions operating on the flanks. The main problem was finding sufficient landing craft to mount the assault, a shortcoming which meant that the operation could not take place until June at the earliest.

At the same time plans were discussed to drive the Japanese out of Burma. In October 1943 Admiral Lord Louis Mountbatten was appointed Supreme Allied Commander South East Asia and his first proposal was to launch an amphibious attack from the Bay of Bengal. This was stymied by a lack of landing craft; meanwhile, sensing that the Allies were planning to mount a major offensive, the Japanese laid plans to attack in northern Burma to cut the Allied communications centre at Imphal in Assam. Mountbatten's response was Operation Thursday: the success of the first Chindit expedition of 1943 had encouraged Wingate to begin planning for a second long-range penetration operation which would take place in the spring of 1944 to coincide with an assault made by Chinese forces under the command of the US General Joseph Stillwell to retake and secure northern Burma.

BURMA

1st battalion

This new Chindit force, known as 3rd Indian Infantry Division to deceive the Japanese, consisted of six infantry brigades (twice the size of a normal division) and 1st Cameronians formed 111 Brigade with 2nd King's Own Royal Regiment and 3/4th and 4/9th Gurkha Rifles, all under the command of Brigadier W. D. A. 'Joe' Lentaigne. Each battalion was divided into two columns, the Cameronians' being numbered 26 and 90 to reflect the regiment's history. Basically, a Chindit column was a reinforced rifle company of 250 men consisting of four infantry platoons, a heavy weapons platoon equipped with a Vickers .303 medium machine gun and three-inch mortar, a commando platoon, a reconnaissance platoon and a section of guides provided by the Burma Rifles. Training began in earnest in August 1943 with the intention that two brigades (77 and 111) would be flown in by air to create 'strongholds' at positions known as Broadway and Piccadilly while 16 Brigade under Brigadier Bernard Fergusson would march into the Indaw area from Ledo in the north. When Lieutenant-Colonel John Masters, a Gurkha officer who was later to replace Lentaigne, came to write his memoirs, he produced a telling description of the men who had been chosen to do battle against the Japanese in the fastness of the Burmese jungle:

> They recruited most of their men from the streets of Glasgow, and had the reputation of being one of the toughest regiments in the British Army, in peacetime. They waged street fights with secreted bayonets and broken bottles, and, on at least one occasion in Calcutta, with rifles and ball ammunition. They carried razor blades in the peaks of their caps, with which to wipe the grin off opposing faces by a careless back swipe from the bonnet; and potatoes in their pockets, in which razor blades were stuck. No one but their own officers could handle them, and their touchy discipline vanished altogether for a week around the great Scottish fiesta of Hogmanay, New Year's Eve.

Masters was also astute enough to notice that Wingate caused considerable offence to the battalion while it was training in Gwalior. Wingate was steeped in the language of the Old Testament – he counted Plymouth Brethren and the Free Church of Scotland amongst the influences on his background – and with his beard and Wolseley helmet he cut an eccentric, almost prophet-like figure. It was his habit to visit units in training and to give talks which were peppered with biblical allusions. However, when he addressed

1st Cameronians Wingate made the mistake of telling them that many would perish in the attempt to retake Burma and as related by Masters this was badly received by the men: 'I could sense an almost visible rising of the regimental esprit de corps against the general. The regiment decided he was trying to frighten them into bravery, and the real worth of Wingate's remarks – a message about sacrifice – was lost.'

Operation Thursday is one of the great imponderables of the Second World War. Despite problems with reconnaissance the fly-in was a success and on 9 March over 9,000 men, 1,500 mules and all the force's equipment and arms had landed by glider behind Japanese lines. Two days later, in a colourful Order of the Day, Wingate exulted that 'all our columns are inserted in the enemy's guts . . . Let us thank God for the great success He has vouchsafed us, and press forward with our sword in the enemy's ribs to expel him from our territory.' Both 77 and 111 Brigades had achieved their objectives, the former by marching towards Mawlu and the latter by crossing the Irrawaddy. However, problems were already beginning to mount. Having flown into Broadway, Lentaigne was forced to abandon the proposed stronghold at Chowringhee because it proved too difficult to defend and delays in crossing the Irrawaddy put his brigade behind schedule. It was not until 26 March that it reached Wuntho. Difficulties also arose over the deployment of 14 and 23 Brigades, which were supposed to be flown in as reinforcements: due to threatened Japanese moves towards Imphal, General William Slim, commanding Fourteenth Army, wanted to keep them as strategic reserves.

It was then that disaster struck. On 24 March Wingate was killed in an air crash when his US Army Air Force B-25 Mitchell bomber crashed into the jungle while he was flying from Imphal to Lalaghat. All on board were killed and at one stroke the Chindits had lost their inspirational leader. As the cipher officer of 111

Brigade put it: 'Our master was gone and we, his masterpiece, were now ownerless.' From this point onwards, with the force still engaged in hard fighting behind enemy lines, the Chindit concept began to unravel. A successor had to be found and, as the senior brigadier, Lentaigne was appointed to take Wingate's place. One of his first appointments was Colonel Henry Alexander, a Cameronian, as his chief of staff. To meet the new circumstances, at a specially convened conference on 27 March it was decided to employ the Chindits to attack the lines of communication of the Japanese Fifteenth Army and the task was given to 14 and 111 Brigade, the latter now under Masters' temporary command.

Six days later there was another change when Slim cancelled the orders and decided to put the Chindits under the operational command of General Joseph Stillwell, US Army, who was operating to the north with the Chinese National Army. Lentaigne moved his headquarters to Shaduzup to be closer to his new commanders and the Chindit brigades were realigned. All their positions were abandoned and a new block was established at a position called Blackpool, north of Indaw on the main road and rail routes between Mogaung and Myitkyina. First to arrive was 111 Brigade, which reached the position on 7 May and immediately began reinforcing its inadequate defences. By then there were powerful Japanese forces at divisional strength in the area and Blackpool came under immediate and sustained attack. At the end of May the battalion withdrew to Indawgyi Lake, where it was re-supplied by flying boats which also evacuated the growing number of casualties to India. As the regimental history describes, the onset of the monsoon created added hazards for the men:

> The mud on the hills was indescribable, many of the slopes were very steep, and the jungle in places almost impenetrable. Moreover, the privations of the past three

months had left the survivors of the Battalion in poor physical condition. Most had lost weight, many were extremely emaciated, and the rough going proved so hard on the feet that there were few who were not lame in a few days. Several of the animals [mules] became unfit for work owing to exhaustion and had to be destroyed.

In fact the Chindits' fate had already been sealed by putting them under Stillwell's command. Not only was the US general a committed Anglophobe whose dislike of the British was almost pathological, but he used the Chindit columns as ordinary infantry without armoured or artillery support, a role for which they had not been trained. Fighting in support of the US–Chinese forces in the Mogaung–Myitkyina area they gave a fine account of themselves in spite of suffering heavy casualties but they were wasted in that role. Following Wingate's untimely death it would have been more sensible to withdraw them and to re-form them for another of the long-range penetration operations for which they had been specially trained and equipped. At the end of August that decision was finally taken and, physically and mentally exhausted, they were ordered to withdraw to India. By then, 1st Cameronians had been reduced to a cadre and was no longer considered capable of taking part in offensive operations. In July the battalion was withdrawn and it took the better part of a week to march out of Burma. The survivors had been in the field for five months, two more than had originally been planned, and, as Masters noted, most of the men in the brigade were badly demoralised and had become 'convinced that Stillwell meant to murder us'. At the beginning of 1945 the Chindits were officially disbanded and in August that same year the war in Burma came to a victorious conclusion after the Fourteenth Army smashed the Japanese at Imphal, Kohma and Meiktila before advancing on Mandalay and Rangoon.

Because Wingate died at a crucial juncture in the operation and was unable to influence future events it is difficult to give a complete estimate of the achievements of 1st Cameronians and the other battalions which served as Chindits. The force lost 1,034 casualties killed and 2,752 wounded (Cameronian losses were 10 officers killed or wounded and 237 other ranks killed or wounded), but against that they accounted for over 10,000 casualties in the Japanese army, 5,764 of whom were killed. The Chindits also suffered dreadful privations from illness and lack of food and came out of Burma a much-weakened and emaciated force, but the battlefield accountancy should not just be confined to figures. After landing in Burma they had operated freely against the enemy's lines of communication and sowed confusion in the minds of Japanese commanders, who were never entirely certain of the force's whereabouts or intentions. As a result a large number of troops were used in countering the threat, including one reserve division and two battalions which would otherwise have been used in the army attacking Imphal and Kohima. In that respect the suffering endured by 1st Cameronians made a substantial contribution to the success of the Allied war effort in Burma.

ITALY

2nd battalion

By the end of 1943 Italy had surrendered and the Allies had invaded the country through Reggio Calabria and Salerno. Naples, too, had fallen but the Allies' attempts to move quickly on Rome had been blocked by the Germans along the Gustav Line with the result that offensives were confined to the coastal flanks. In the centre the mountainous terrain and obstacles such as the rivers Garigliano and Liri made any advance difficult and hopes for an early breakthrough quickly faded. It was a country which favoured those defending it and the difficulties were exacerbated by the foul winter weather, which hindered offensive operations. To break the impasse it was decided to mount an amphibious operation which would land Allied forces at Anzio behind the German defensive positions. Codenamed Operation Shingle, the idea was to use General John P. Lucas's US VI Corps (1st British Infantry Division and 3rd US Infantry Division plus Commando and Ranger forces) to secure a beach-head and then to threaten the road to Rome, which lay 30 miles to the north. Unfortunately, Lucas then dithered, waiting for the build-up of his forces to be completed, and this allowed the Germans to react. When he eventually attempted to move inland at the end of January the way had been blocked and US VI Corps found itself stuck on the Anzio salient.

By the end of January the US had sustained 3,000 casualties and the British 2,100, although the 1st Division had managed to fight its way towards Osteriaccia. Determined to block the Allies at all costs, the Germans pushed more forces into the area under the command of General Eberhard von Mackensen, but a fresh assault in mid-February was beaten by VI Corps, now under the command of Lieutenant-General Lucian Truscott. Amongst the forces used to reinforce the Anzio bridgehead was the 5th Division, which had been transferred to the command of the Fifth Army. On arrival in the Anzio beachhead on 10 March 2nd Cameronians was given the responsibility for a front known as the 'Fortress', situated on the north side of the beachhead perimeter. It proved to be a tense time, with raids and counter-raids on the German positions and a steady loss of casualties. The stalemate was broken on 25 May when news arrived that elements of VI Corps had broken through the German defences to meet up with the rapidly advancing Fifth Army and that as a result the road to Rome was now open. (For 2nd Cameronians the first indication of change had come when patrols found that the Fortress was clear of German troops and they were able to enter it unopposed.) Within a week the 2nd battalion had occupied Castle Porziano about 12 miles south of the city; it was the first British battalion to reach the River Tiber but political considerations obliged the US forces to enter Rome first on 5 June. A week later the battalion was in the city and during its stay Roman Catholic soldiers were invited to a special mass in St Peter's. At the end of the month the 5th Division was removed from the line to re-form near Naples before moving to Taranto prior to a proposed deployment in Palestine and Syria.

FRANCE AND NORTH-WEST EUROPE
2nd, 6th, 7th, 9th battalions

Following the setbacks of 1940 the regiment's three Territorial infantry battalions had spent their war in Britain training for the time when the Allies would be able to take the war back to Nazi Germany on the European mainland. While the 9th battalion served in 15th (Scottish) Division, being brigaded with 2nd Glasgow Highlanders and 7th Seaforth Highlanders, the 6th and 7th battalions trained in the mountain warfare role with 52nd (Lowland) Division. This latter formation had a chequered career: following its brief foray in Normandy in 1940 it trained as a mountain warfare division for a proposed invasion of Norway, then it retrained as an air support division for the airborne operations at Arnhem in September 1944 before finally going into action below sea level during the operations at Walcheren to retake the Scheldt estuary in November. Its 156 Brigade comprised both the Cameronian battalions and 4/5th Royal Scots Fusiliers, and was often referred to as the Cameronian Brigade.

First to go into action in mainland Europe was 9th Cameronians, which was destined to be in continuous active service from June 1944 until the end of the war 11 months later. As a result its casualties were the highest in the regiment – during the Second World War The Cameronians (Scottish Rifles) lost a total of 1,222 soldiers killed in action. The battalion landed at Arromanches on 17 June and was immediately in action. Two weeks after the initial D-Day landings the Allied attack had stalled, with the Germans still defending the town of Caen, preventing any movement towards the open ground around Falaise. Montgomery's response was to use three newly arrived divisions, including 15th (Scottish), to make the attack towards the high ground east of the River Orne in order to envelop the city and sweep up its defenders. The operation was codenamed Epsom and it began on 26 June with the 15th (Scottish) Division in the vanguard, moving forward with 700 infantrymen backed by artillery and armoured support provided by 11th Armoured Division and 31 Tank Brigade. Poor weather conditions with heavy rain meant that there would only be limited air cover and when 9th Cameronians went into the attack a hail storm began and the drizzle continued throughout the day as the division pushed towards the small town of Cheux. Before the 9th battalion began its attack one of the company commanders noticed that a planning error would lead to his outer flank coming under 'friendly fire' from Allied artillery, but it proved impossible to make any changes to the plan and many of his riflemen were killed or wounded in the opening barrage. Casualties were carefully marked by upturned rifles and one observer quoted in John Keegan's history of the campaign remembered the poignancy of seeing 'these rifles surmounted by their tin helmets looking like strange fungi sprouting up haphazardly through cornfields'. During the operation the battalion reached its objective, the village of Haut du Bosq, but in the process suffered 120 casualties killed and wounded.

The fighting continued for a week before the division was withdrawn without achieving the expected breakthrough. Although Epsom was not a tactical success, it had taken the sting out of the German counter-attack and prevented German armour from driving a wedge between the Allied forces as they forced their way south into Normandy. While these events were unfolding the stalemate was broken by Operation Cobra, mounted on 25 July by the US First Army, which pushed as far south as Avranches and the pivotal neighbouring town of Pontaubault. Suddenly the possibility opened up of invading Brittany in the west and racing eastwards toward Le Mans and the River Seine. The task was given to seven divisions of Patton's US Third Army, which moved with exemplary speed through the Avranches–Pontaubault gap; the break-out from Normandy had finally begun and the Allies were free to sweep east and threaten the Seine valley and the approaches to Paris.

On 28 August 9th Cameronians passed over the Seine in broad daylight and a week later it had crossed the border into Belgium where it followed, in reverse, the route taken by the 2nd battalion during the retreat to Dunkirk. Amongst those who had taken part, as a young officer, in that unhappy episode was the commanding officer Lieutenant-Colonel Sir Edward Bradford. The next point of contact with the Germans was a new defensive line along the River Maas. In a successful attack on 7 September the 9th battalion drove back the Germans on the River Escaut and five days later it had reached the Escaut Canal. This was a prelude to a move into Holland where 9th Cameronians joined 7th Seaforths in the capture of the vital bridgehead at Best on 2 October followed by Tilburg on 27 October – in a countryside dominated by water it was essential to capture and secure the bridges over the various canals and waterways.

Although the rapid advance into the Low Countries had presented huge problems to the Germans, it had also discommoded the Allies by creating difficulties in supply and re-supply. The further they advanced into Europe the further away were the main Channel ports which provided them with much-needed fuel, munitions and the materiel of war. With its huge docks and access to the North Sea, Antwerp was the only port capable of giving them everything they needed but it was still in German control and its seaward approaches were heavily mined. With winter approaching the need to capture Antwerp and to open up the Scheldt estuary was imperative and so it was that the mountain soldiers of the 52nd (Lowland) Division found themselves crossing the Channel in the middle of October to support Canadian forces in a part of Europe which was below sea level.

The 6th and 7th battalions landed at Ostend with 4/5th Royal Scots Fusiliers and immediately regrouped in the nearby town of Deinze near Ghent, where they were equipped with tracked amphibious vehicles known as 'buffaloes', each of which was capable of carrying up to 30 infantrymen. As there were transport shortages 7th Cameronians was kept in reserve and the two-battalion force went into action on 26 October across the West Scheldt. Having landed in South Beveland they soon found themselves caught up in the difficult and dangerous business of fighting in a built-up area. Faced by the onslaught the Germans put up determined resistance and defended stubbornly to protect their positions and before the causeway to Walcheren could be opened the 6th battalion had to undertake the hazardous crossing of the muddy waters of the Slooe Channel – in places the muddy water was over four feet deep. At the same time 7th Cameronians crossed to the north and captured Veere, and as the diary of Jack Rafferty makes clear, the assault was an overwhelming success:

> The Cameronians crossed the channel in assault boats and started up the marked track through the marshes. Reaching firm ground on Walcheren they caught the enemy completely by surprise. The whole bridgehead established on Walcheren was now 2,000 yards deep and two miles wide. At Veere the enemy was so completely shattered by the force of the advance that they came marching in by the

thousand. Companies were sending back prisoners of war many times as strong as the battalions, to be dealt with by the overworked prisoner of war cage personnel.

Walcheren fell on 8 November and the Cameronian brigade's next operation was the advance towards the Rhine. This took them towards the line of the Lower Maas and its flooded sections around 's-Hertogenbosch. At the beginning of December the brigade crossed over the border into Germany on the extreme right of the British line. Still in the Geilenkirchen sector the Cameronian brigade opened its account in 1945 by taking part in Operation Blackcock, an offensive against German positions in the triangle of land between the rivers Maas and Roer. This was a large-scale operation undertaken in bitterly cold conditions, with infantry and armour combining in a nine-day battle which fully tested those who took part in it. Thanks to their training as mountain troops, the men of 52nd (Lowland) Division were properly equipped and were able to withstand the harsh weather conditions. In that role both the Cameronian battalions attacked due east from Sittard along the axis of the southern fringe of the heavily wooded area of Echterbosch. This was a fiercely contested battle in which infantry had to take on and destroy German tanks, including the Tiger with its much-feared 88-mm gun capable of piercing armour at a range of 2,000 metres. During the final stages of the operation, on the night of 22/23 January, the two Cameronian battalions combined in the operation to take the town of Obspringen, where a defensive line was formed and held for the next ten days.

Ahead lay the last great obstacle, the River Rhine, which the Allies approached on a broad front with Montgomery's Twenty-First Army Group being given the formidable task of crossing the lower reaches at Emmerich, Rees, Wesel and Rheinberg, where the river was wider. For the initial assault Montgomery selected

15th (Scottish) Division and 51st (Highland) Division, which both crossed the river at Wesel without too much difficulty on the night of 23 March. The only Cameronian battalion to take part in the operation was 9th Cameronians, which crossed unopposed in buffaloes and moved immediately towards the village of Rees. Once across the river, the way into the Westphalian plain was open but as the German defenders fell back on their fatherland they fought with a growing intensity. Saturation bombing of German towns by the Allied air forces also held up the advance and all the Cameronian battalions found that the dying days of the war in Europe were as difficult as anything they had come across since the D-Day landings in the previous year. And as the war history recorded, the advancing Allied army began to witness the first evidence of the aftermath of war: 'Displaced persons of many Nationalities – Belgians, Dutch, French, Russians and Poles – were to be seen in small groups trekking Westwards with their scanty belongings.'

During the 52nd (Lowland) Division's advance at the beginning of March, 6th Cameronians led the attack on the town of Goch in the Reichswald, where it almost lost its commanding officer Lieutenant-Colonel E. N. Southward when his jeep hit a landmine. Fortunately he was only wounded but it is a measure of the intensity of the fighting in north-west Europe that he was the fourth commanding officer to become a casualty. This was followed on 7 March by an even stiffer battle against German parachute troops on the town of Alpon, which covered the approaches to the Rhine. During the fighting, which lasted until 10 March, 6th Cameronians lost 173 casualties killed and wounded and as a result the battalion's C Company had to be re-formed from scratch. At the same time, in an internal reorganisation of the division, 7th Cameronians transferred to 157 Brigade to take the place of 1st Glasgow Highlanders. Both battalions crossed the Rhine on 29

March and both played their part in the drive into Germany which led to the final collapse of the Nazi government on 8 May.

By 29 April 9th Cameronians was across the River Elbe and heading for the town of Basedow where 240 German prisoners-of-war were taken into custody. Two days later the battalion cleared the Sachsenwald Forest, where news of the impending Armistice was received. By then both 6th and 7th Cameronians had been part of the force that had broken into Bremen at the end of April. Although it had been a satisfying moment the edge was taken off the celebrations when 6th Cameronians entered a camp at Sanbostel halfway between Bremen and Bremerhaven. As the war history recorded, nothing could have prepared the men for their first experience of liberating a concentration camp:

> All around was a flat and desolate plain, and, in the centre, a vast cage, wherein seemed to be confined all the bestialities that even the most fertile imagination could conjure up. Everywhere there was filth and stench and disease and hordes of dehumanised creatures with shrunken faces, cloaking their emaciated bodies in the dirty rags of their striped prison uniform. No one who did not see and smell and feel the horror of this nightmare could ever believe it. And no one who did see it and smell it and feel it could ever forget it.

By then the 2nd battalion had arrived in north-west Europe as part of the reinforcements needed to bring the war to a speedier conclusion. Having been trained for service in the Middle East, in February 1945 it moved to Marseilles, where it was despatched north by train to Belgium. Its last formal action took place on 22 April against German positions in the town of Bleckede. Although the end of the war was now in sight the men in the 2nd battalion noticed that the German defenders continued to fight until further resistance was useless. Only then would they surrender. Usually this was done in groups of 25 or more but on 2 May a whole formation surrendered when the 245th Infantry Regiment capitulated and handed itself over to 2nd Cameronians. By the following day the battalion had reached the Baltic port of Lübeck where it had the satisfaction of taking the surrender of the headquarters staff of the German 27th Corps. Its final move was to Sprenge where it ended the war. After three years, which had seen the battalion serve in the Middle East, Sicily, Italy and north-west Europe, the war for 2nd Cameronians was finally over.

No mention of the Cameronians' war record can omit the service of senior regimental officers who played leading roles in the direction of the war. The most eminent was General Sir Richard O'Connor KT, GCB, DSO, MC (1889–1981), who had been commissioned into the regiment in 1909 and who commanded the Western Defence Force which inflicted a heavy defeat on the Italian army in Libya in 1940. Unfortunately he was taken prisoner the following year and while he managed to escape and returned to command VIII Corps in the fighting in Europe, he was past his best and did not shine. (One of his divisional commanders Major-General G. P. B. Roberts regretted that he 'did not understand the handling of armour on a European battlefield'.) After the war O'Connor was appointed Adjutant-General but resigned on a point of principle in 1947. As O'Connor arrived at the War Office another Cameronian general was leaving – this was General Sir Thomas Riddell-Webster GCB, DSO, DL (1886–1974), who served as a highly successful Quartermaster-General from 1942 to 1946. Earlier in his career he had commanded 2nd Scottish Rifles. The third full general was Sir Horatius Murray GCB, KBE, CB, DSO (1903–1989), who commanded 153 Brigade at the Battle of El Alamein and who went on to command 6th Armoured Division in the fighting in

Europe. After the war he commanded 1st Division in Palestine and the Commonwealth Division in Korea, and ended his army career as Commander-in-Chief Allied Forces, North Europe. The historian Philip Grant has also made a case for including General Sir Roy Bucher KBE, CB, MC, DL (1895–1980), who although a cavalryman began his career in the regiment in 1915 and succeeded O'Connor as Commander-in-Chief Eastern Command in India.

Other notable Cameronian generals are: Lieutenant-General Sir John Evetts CB, CBE, MC (1891–1988), who commanded 6th Division in Syria and ended the war as Assistant Chief of the Imperial General Staff with responsibility for weapons procurement; Lieutenant-General Sir Alexander Galloway KBE, CB, DSO, MC (1895–1977), who commanded 1st Cameronians at the outbreak of war and seemed destined for a glittering operational career before, to his dismay, he was returned to the War Office as Director of Staff Duties in 1943; Lieutenant-General Sir George Collingwood KBE, CB, DSO (1903–1986), who commanded 10th Highland Light Infantry in 1942 and 33 Indian Brigade in Burma from 1944 to 1945; Major-General Robin Murray CB, MC (1888–1985), who commanded 15th (Scottish Division) 1940–1941; Major-General Douglas Graham CB, CBE, DSO, MC, DL (1893–1971), who commanded 153 Brigade in North Africa and 50th (Northumbrian) Division in Europe in 1944; Major-General Eric Sixsmith CB, CBE (1904–1986), who commanded 2nd Royal Scots Fusiliers in Italy and 2nd Cameronians in 1944; Major-General John Frost CB, DSO, MC (1912–1993), who won undying fame commanding 2nd Parachute Regiment during the ill-fated Arnhem operation in 1944; and Major-General Henry Alexander CB, CBE, DSO (1912–1977), who commanded 2nd Scottish Rifles in Italy and served as Brigadier General Staff during the second Chindit operation of 1944.

TEN

Peace and Disbandment

Britain and its Allies had won the war but the task of reconstruction was to be a complicated, time-consuming and, above all, expensive business. Many of the earlier economic problems from the 1930s remained and had been exacerbated by the six years of conflict. Overseas investments had been sold off, the country's infrastructure, including five million houses, had been badly damaged by enemy bombing and in the course of fighting the war 18 million tons of merchant shipping had been lost. In an attempt to reduce the scale of the debt and to find finance for post-war reconstruction the new Labour government had to apply to the US for a loan of $3,750 million, and this was only achieved by undertaking to restore the convertibility of sterling at the earliest possible date. Inevitably the new financial arrangements made the country ever more dependent on the dollar and this connection was mirrored in foreign policy. In 1949 the North Atlantic Treaty Organisation (NATO) came into being as the West's main defensive alliance to counter the growing threat produced by the Soviet Union and its Warsaw Pact allies. By then the wartime alliance had collapsed and following the blockade of Berlin in 1948 the confrontation between NATO and the Soviet Union became increasingly bitter and belligerent. As a result the British Army of the Rhine (BAOR) was created, with its primary combat formation 1 British Corps consisting of one infantry division and three armoured divisions plus supporting services. This was Britain's contribution to the post-war defence of western Europe during the period which came to be known as the Cold War, and for the rest of the century West Germany was to be a second home for the regiment, as it was for every other regiment in the British Army.

Despite the need to garrison western Germany and the continuing military presence in the colonial empire, the post-war years also brought a contraction in the size of the army. Given the rapid wartime expansion – between 1939 and 1945 it had swollen to 5.1 million soldiers – this was perhaps inevitable and it followed a pattern of growth and decline which had been familiar in the previous two centuries. For the infantry this meant the disappearance of some time-honoured formations and each decade from the 1940s through to the end of the century saw a steady haemorrhage of regiments from the Army List. The first step was to scrap the Cardwell/Childers' system of linked battalions. With the end of British rule in India in 1947, and the realisation that the empire would be shrinking, there was no longer any need to maintain the concept of home and overseas battalions. As a result all 64 infantry regiments were ordered to reduce to a single battalion; only the three senior foot guards regiments (Grenadier, Coldstream and Scots) and the Parachute Regiment, raised during the war, were excepted from the rule. As a result 1st Cameronians was placed in suspended animation, a move which meant that in theory it could be re-raised, although the War Office discouraged this possibility. At the same time, by a process of amalgamation, in 1948, the 2nd battalion became the new 1st Battalion, The Cameronians (Scottish

Rifles). The reforms were accompanied by the creation of 15 administrative brigades based on a category or regional structure. For Scotland this produced the Lowland Brigade, to which 1st Cameronians was assigned, and the Highland Brigade. Later, each brigade had its own common cap badge, which was worn by all battalions, and for a short time regimental cap badges disappeared. Change was also the order of the day for the wartime Territorial battalions: in 1947 the 6th battalion merged with its duplicate 10th battalion as did the 7th with the 9th. Three years later the 6th and 7th battalions were amalgamated to form 6/7th Battalion The Cameronians (Scottish Rifles).

The other great change in defence policy was the continuation of wartime conscription with the passing of a number of National Service Acts which obliged every able-bodied man to register at his local branch of the Ministry of Labour and National Service as soon as he became 18. Information about the relevant age groups and clear-cut instructions were placed in the national newspapers and broadcast on BBC radio, and schools and employers passed on the relevant official information to their young charges. Short of deliberately refusing to register there was no way the call-up could be ignored and those who did try to avoid conscription were always traced through their National Health records. Between the end of the war and the final phasing-out of conscription in 1963, 2.3 million men served as National Servicemen, the majority in the army. In its final form the period of conscription was two years (there had been earlier periods of 12 and 18 months) and like every other regiment in the British Army The Cameronians benefited from the contribution made by men who were the first peacetime conscripts in British history.

At the conclusion of the fighting in north-west Europe the Cameronians had four battalions in Germany (2nd, 6th, 7th and 9th), where they formed part of the Allied army of occupation. While the onset of peace brought relief and the duties were far from onerous the regimental history records that 'life became more irksome and it was not easy to maintain the enthusiasm and high standard of discipline required of troops in occupation of a defeated enemy country'. Men were demobilised as quickly as was feasible but in so doing old friendships were broken up and the novelty of peacetime Germany quickly waned. Towards the end of 1945 2nd Cameronians moved to Wismar and then to Goslar, which was close to the Russian zone, and this was followed by a tour of duty as the demonstration battalion at the School of Infantry at Warminster. Preparations were then made for a deployment to Gibraltar, which would begin in January 1947. For the Territorial battalions the end of the war also involved them in the normal duties of an army of occupation. The 6th battalion was based variously at Delmenhorst, Magdeburg, the Ruhr and Wilhelmshaven, where it disbanded on 29 October 1946. The 7th battalion spent time tracking down prominent Nazis in the Bremen area before moving to Epselkamp north of Lübbecke, where it disbanded on 19 August 1946. The 9th battalion moved north to Kiel to occupy the port before moving to Bargteheide between Hamburg and Lübeck, where it disbanded on 24 June 1946. For 1st Cameronians there was a different fate: at the conclusion of hostilities in the Far East it was in India, and in November that same year it moved to Singapore, where it was employed on guard and ceremonial duties. At the end of 1946 came the news that the battalion was to be placed in suspended animation as a result of the reduction of infantry battalions (see above) and its remaining members dispersed to other units, the majority choosing 1st Queen's Own Cameron Highlanders.

1ST CAMERONIANS (SCOTTISH RIFLES) 1948–68

The new battalion began its existence in Buena Vista Barracks in Gibraltar under the command of Lieutenant-Colonel Eric

Brickman, in later life the secretary of the prestigious Royal and Ancient Golf Club in St Andrews. At the time the battalion consisted of three rifle companies, a headquarter company and a support company with a total of around 600 men, most of them National Servicemen. At the end of 1948 the battalion transferred to Trieste as part of a UN force to safeguard the region while boundaries were being redrawn in the aftermath of the war. The tour of duty ended a year later, when the battalion moved to Hong Kong on board the troopship *Lancashire*. When it called in to Hong Kong there was an opportunity to make contact with one of the affiliated regiments, 7th Gurkha Rifles, which was given permission for its pipers to wear Douglas tartan plaids. Landfall in Hong Kong was made shortly before the end of 1949. On arrival the battalion joined 26 Gurkha Infantry Brigade as part of 40th Division and it immediately began training in defensive operations for the protection of the Crown Colony – at that time thought to be under threat of attack from neighbouring Communist China.

In fact the battalion was destined to fight a very different kind of war in Malaya to the south. During the Second World War the country had been over-run and captured by the Japanese army, who then garrisoned it with 100,000 troops. The only opposition came from mainly Malay-Chinese guerrilla groups which mounted a limited number of attacks against Japanese installations with the support of Force 136, a British-backed counter-insurgency group. At the end of the war this Malayan People's Anti-Japanese Army was transformed into the Malayan Races Liberation Army (MRLA), which was the military wing of the Chinese-controlled Malayan Communist Party (MCP). Initially Britain planned a Malayan Union which would have given the Chinese citizenship rights but this was opposed by the Malay political elite and the result was the creation of a Malayan Federation in which Chinese rights were sacrificed to the interests of the Malay rulers. As a result of the heightened political tensions the Chinese Communists' opposition turned into an armed struggle in 1948, the MCP was declared illegal and some 10,000 MRLA fighters moved into the jungle to mount guerrilla operations against the civilian population and the security forces under their military commander, Chin Peng.

At the beginning of April 1950 the battalion left for Singapore and immediately began a rigorous programme of jungle warfare training at the Nee Soon Camp while junior officers and NCOs were despatched to the Jungle Warfare Training Centre at Johore Bahru for intensive three-week courses. In May the battalion moved to Johore to take over from 1st Seaforth Highlanders. Initially the idea had been to drive the terrorists (known as CTs, for 'Communist Terrorists') into the jungle away from urban populations but this changed with the appointment of Lieutenant-General Sir Harold Briggs as Director of Operations 'to plan, co-ordinate and to direct the anti-bandit operations of the police and fighting services'. To achieve those ends Briggs integrated the efforts of the police and the military and reorganised the intelligence services to provide him with information about terrorist movements and to infiltrate the Communist cadre infrastructure. A 'food denial' policy was also instituted but the main obstacle was the support given to the MRLA by the Chinese inhabitants of the jungle. The solution was the resettlement of 650,000 villagers in 550 New Villages – secure areas where they would enjoy a safe and profitable environment away from MRLA influence. Then it was the task of the infantry to move into the jungle, to secure bases and drive the CTs into the deeper and less hospitable depths. As the men of 1st Cameronians discovered – the description was given by Major P. K. Bryceson in a BBC radio broadcast in September 1953 – these operations demanded strength, stamina and determination and only the very fittest were able to withstand the rigours of the environment:

> I had served in Burma during the war and expected to
> be fairly familiar with the jungle. But neither the jungles
> nor the enemy could bear comparison with my Burma
> experiences. The Malayan jungle is far more dense and
> difficult to negotiate, and the jungle swamp is so treacherous
> that at one moment you may be stepping on comparatively
> firm ground, then with the next step you sink up to the
> waist in evil-smelling mud and have to be hauled out by
> toggle ropes.

Initially the battalion was in a 'white' area, one that was
considered to be free of terrorists and contacts were infrequent.
As a result longer patrols were made into the jungle, lasting up to
six weeks, and greater efforts were made in building up reliable
intelligence. Air supply was essential and company commanders
often used Auster aircraft for reconnaissance flights. Orders from
headquarters insisted that on patrol officers should not lead from
the front but this was disregarded by the commanding officer,
Lieutenant-Colonel W. M. Henning, and the regimental history
records that 'the most effective Cameronian platoon commanders
led their men from the front'. It was not the only edict from
on high to be cheerfully disregarded. Throughout the campaign
the various infantry battalions in Malaya kept a record of 'kills'
and the Cameronians' record was 125, the second-highest score
during the period of the emergency. (The 'winners' were 1st
Suffolk Regiment with 198 kills, but other regiments complained
that this had only been achieved by creating special 'hit squads'.)
However, in 1952 a visiting Member of Parliament declared the
custom barbaric – there was an unofficial league table – and
the practice was banned. The Cameronians' own losses were 23
officers and men killed in action or died on active service.

During the summer of 1951 the battalion moved from Muar

to the Segamat area of Johore at a time when overall command in Malaya was assumed by General Sir Gerald Templer, who refined the tactics and introduced a stronger political element. His credo was expressed in a statement he used over and over again: 'The shooting side of the business is only 25 per cent of the trouble, the other 75 per cent is getting the people of this country behind us.' The MCP had launched the insurgency to gain independence for Malaya but successive federal and state elections were held from 1952 with the aim of achieving that ambition. This policy encouraged moderate politicians but as the communists were excluded from the process they were gradually sidelined and independence was eventually granted in August 1957. Even so, military operations continued unabated, with a new emphasis on deep jungle patrolling and the introduction of psychological warfare with intensive propaganda to undermine MRLA morale. During these operations 1st Cameronians was helped by Iban trackers from Borneo; in time there were sufficient to form a platoon and the regimental magazine *The Covenanter* recorded that 'they all deserve the name of Cameronians'. The account added a telling description of their skills: 'They knew all about the jungle and were expert trackers; their skill was uncanny when tracking, and when the scent was hot, they went faster than any hunting dog.'

In April 1953 the tour of duty came to an end and 1st Cameronians returned to Britain on the troopship *Empire Halladale*. It had been a huge success, the battalion had proved itself to be a fine fighting formation and morale was high: the next trick was to make sure that those virtues were carried over into the very different conditions of peacetime soldiering at the next station at Barnard Castle in County Durham. For a time there was a dramatic slump when spirits sank but matters improved in May 1954 when the battalion moved to its first deployment with BAOR, taking over Spey Barracks in Buxtehude from 1st Seaforth Highlanders.

PEACE AND DISBANDMENT

As part of 7th Armoured Division the battalion began training in support of tanks, the mentors being 8th King's Royal Irish Hussars. The battalion quickly settled down to the different routines of the BAOR training year and, as the regimental history recorded, 'it was apparent that the Barnard Castle period – uneasy and at times shabby – was over'. Locally the pipes and drums were in constant demand and during the summer of 1955 the battalion enjoyed its best performance at Bisley since the 1930s.

At the beginning of 1957 there was a 'first' for the battalion when it was despatched by air for its next deployment in Bahrain, where it was tasked to guard local oil pipelines at a time of unrest in the Persian Gulf. It turned out to be a roundabout trip. Planes carrying an average of 50 men each left Blackbushe and Stansted airports at regular intervals bound for the first halt at Tripoli in Libya. From there they carried on to Kano in Nigeria or Banqui in French Equatorial Africa (later Central African Republic) before flying first to Entebbe in Uganda and then on to Aden. (During the stop at Kano the commanding officer, Lieutenant-Colonel D. M. Carter-Campbell, was astonished to be greeted by Lieutenant-Colonel Moir Stormonth-Darling, a well-known Cameronian commanding a battalion of the Nigeria Regiment, who had made a long and difficult journey to see his old regiment. Later, after retiring from the Regular Army, he commanded 5th Black Watch.)

Oil had been discovered in Bahrain in 1932, and the island kingdom had been close to Britain, but anti-British sentiments in the post-war world led to local rioting and the deployment of additional troops, including 1st Cameronians. The deployment also gave the battalion its first taste of the unsettled political scene in southern Arabia when it was sent to maintain order in the Trucial Oman States at the request of the Sultan of Muscat and Oman. The main operation involved the use of land and air forces to retake Nizwa, a strategically important town in the interior, and this involved D Company and Support Company in some fierce fighting near the village of Firq. Although in theory the companies were not allowed to take a leading role and were supposed to be acting in support of Arab troops, both were obliged to defend themselves from rebel fire. On the night of 10 August patrols of 15/19 Hussars probed the opposition positions and found them to be stronger than expected. As a result the two Cameronian companies mounted a dawn raid in support of the Trucial Oman Scouts. Nizwa duly fell but because of political considerations most of the British forces, including 1st Cameronians, were withdrawn in September. The battalion's casualties were light – 19 men succumbed to, but recovered from, heat stroke.

Following the Oman deployment, which proved to be a mixed experience, the battalion moved to Kenya for a tour of duty which began in May 1958. Almost immediately it was put on 24 hours notice to move due to a sudden and dangerous deterioration in the political affairs of the Middle East. First came a coup d'etat in Iraq on 15 July, which saw the Hashemite King Feisal deposed and replaced by Brigadier Abdul Karim Kassem, and this was followed by an appeal from King Hussein of Jordan for British military assistance. The king's call for help was genuine enough: Feisal was his cousin and anti-Hashemite feeling was rife throughout the Middle East. As Jordan was an important ally the British government responded immediately by ordering the deployment of 16 Independent Parachute Brigade Group. Fortuitously, it had been training in Cyprus for a possible intervention in Lebanon, which was also on the brink of civil war. The following day, 17 July, 1st Cameronians was also ordered to Jordan to join the Parachute Brigade and the first part of the journey was undertaken in a variety of RAF transport aircraft which flew the battalion to Aden. For a hot three weeks the battalion remained in the uncomfortable transit camp at Khormaksar before embarking on the carrier HMS

Bulwark and the frigate HMS *Ulysses* to Aqaba, where its task was protection of the airfield. The battalion was eventually withdrawn at the end of the year and returned to Kenya, where it remained on permanent stand-by until February 1960.

Following home leave in Scotland the battalion's next tour of duty took it back to BAOR, where its base was Elizabeth Barracks in Minden. Unfortunately for the regiment's reputation, the deployment was marred by an incident in April 1962 when there was a mass fight in the local Coliseum bar between German youths and soldiers from the battalion. Once it had been broken up 17 soldiers were arrested and two of them were sent for court martial. At the time the fight attracted little interest – squabbles between BAOR soldiers and Germans were commonplace – but a few months later the British press took up the story. During the investigations the word 'Giftzwerg' (poison dwarf) was used by some of the locals to describe Cameronian soldiers and it stuck. It has to be said, too, that within the battalion it caused no little amusement and was even regarded as a compliment, but the adverse publicity was harmful. It mattered not that 1st Cameronians had engaged itself on local community projects; for the press all that seemed to count was a bar room brawl which had achieved a widespread notoriety. The tour of duty came to an end in the spring of 1964 when the battalion returned to Scotland to undertake public duties in Edinburgh.

The last of these duties took place on 16 March 1966, when a Guard of Honour was provided for the Lord Lyon King of Arms to announce the dissolution of parliament. Six weeks later the battalion was in Aden to replace 1st King's Own Yorkshire Light Infantry on internal security duties. During the steam age the port had been a vital coaling station on the sea route to India through the Suez Canal, and following the Suez debacle it became a major military base and the headquarters of Middle East Command. There had already been outbreaks of trouble in the Radfan hinterland earlier in the decade and by the time the battalion arrived there was a state of virtual civil war between the two opposing factions – the National Liberation Front (NLF) and the Front for the Liberation of South Yemen (FLOSY). From the outset the commanding officer, Lieutenant-Colonel D. B. Riddell-Webster, insisted that there should never be any indiscriminate firing and that the local population should be treated with due courtesy at all times.

In carrying out internal security duties a high premium was placed on patrolling, both on foot and mounted in Land Rovers; at the same time the battalion had to maintain itself and this concentration of duties meant that everyone had to work hard without hope of getting much spare time. Then there was the stifling heat and the constant danger of terrorist attack – during its deployment the battalion suffered over 100 assaults by hand grenade. As an article in *The Covenanter* made clear, vigilance was essential:

> It is of the utmost importance that the soldier in Aden should develop a sense of alertness. There is absolutely no telling when an attack may come, and each and every man has to learn how to react automatically to the shout of 'Grenade!' He must learn too that once the grenade has landed, he must hurl himself to the ground (if not already there), or take such appropriate action as may be necessary to locate the thrower, and then to shoot or capture him, or to take the number of his getaway vehicle. To this end, constant drills are practised, especially anti-grenade drills, where everyone throws himself to the ground, feet first towards the point of burst. If this is done, there is not only every chance of survival, but very small chance of being wounded.

PEACE AND DISBANDMENT

On 18 January 1967 the first terrorist was killed in Aden city after throwing a grenade at a Cameronian patrol, and a week later Rifleman Charles McLaren of B Company was killed in the streets. Happily it was not all work and no play. During the Christmas and New Year period of 1966–67 the battalion celebrated in traditional style with plenty of drink, the regimental history noting with admiration that 'all the older officers and NCOs agreed that never before had they seen such quantities consumed without a fight developing at some stage'. And then, a few weeks later, shortly before the battalion was due to leave, the pipes and drums performed the Beating of Retreat, which was generally agreed to be one of the best in the regiment's history. By the end of February 1967 the battalion had returned to Britain and with them they brought the praise of Major-General Sir John Willoughby, GOC Middle East Land Forces, who wrote to the Chief of the General Staff, General Sir James Cassels, expressing his admiration for the regiment in glowing terms:

> The men arrived in the heat of summer with all the appearances and bearing of troops seasoned in the kind of half-war we wage here.
>
> They went straight on patrols and escorts; and from the day of their first appearance they looked like business. They have never looked otherwise.
>
> And in many ways a much less easy reputation to earn under these trying conditions, they have won a name for exceptional courtesy. They will ever be remembered by the families of servicemen and civilians with affection, not only for these qualities but in their crowning of their association with their Pipes in the open streets. And in the telling of this day by the ordinary wives of ordinary families bearing the strains of terrorism I have seen tears of gratitude and of pride.

The pleasant afterglow provided by a successful tour of duty did not last very long. By the time the 1st battalion returned from Aden further change in the army's structure was on the way as a result of the need to impose additional economies at a point when Britain's strategic interests were changing focus. The ending of National Service (see above) in 1957 and the introduction of a professional all-volunteer force was also a driver of change. During the period of conscription the army had maintained 20 armoured regiments in addition to the 64 infantry regiments and supporting arms and it was clear that there would be insufficient volunteers to fill their ranks. It was agreed, therefore, that the infantry should be reduced by selecting 15 pairs of regiments from the brigade structure to bring each brigade down to four battalions. In Scotland The Highland Light Infantry was transferred to the Lowland Brigade and amalgamated with The Royal Scots Fusiliers to form The Royal Highland Fusiliers. Elsewhere, after 1962, 'large regiments' were formed, such as The Royal Anglian Regiment, which consisted of four battalions representing the following old English county regiments – Royal Norfolk, Suffolk, Cambridgeshire, Royal Lincolnshire, Royal Leicestershire, Northamptonshire, Bedfordshire and Hertfordshire and Essex. It was a process which caused a great deal of sadness and heartache and gave rise to a belief that the system should be scrapped entirely and replaced by a Corps of Infantry with numbered regiments and a central pool of reinforcements. That idea was stoutly resisted and in 1968 the brigade structure disappeared, along with the much disliked cap badges, and was replaced by the formation of six administrative divisions – Guards, Scottish, Queen's, King's, Prince of Wales's and Light. It was a structure which Wellington might have recognised.

Throughout this process The Cameronians had remained unscathed despite suggestions that as the junior regiment in the

Lowland Brigade it was now living on borrowed time. In 1964 a Labour administration came to power under Prime Minister Harold Wilson, with Denis Healey as Secretary of State for Defence. One of its first actions was to begin a Defence Review to consider policy in the light of the country's difficult economic circumstances and the reduction in colonial commitments east of Suez. For the regiment this meant losing its depot at Lanark and the loss of its Territorial battalion, which was reduced to company size in the re-formed Territorial Army and Volunteer Reserve. (Its parent regiment was 52nd Lowland Volunteers.) A second election in 1966, also won by Labour, hastened the process of change still further and the worsening economic situation made additional cuts in the armed forces inevitable. Although expensive projects such as the TSR-2 strike aircraft and CVA-01 fleet carriers were cancelled the army was made to bear the brunt of the manpower cuts, with a reduction in strength from 200,000 to 165,000: this entailed the loss of four armoured, four artillery, one engineer and eight infantry regiments. Amongst the latter was 1st Cameronians.

Amalgamation with another regiment in the Lowland Brigade was one option and it was also one that had already been taken in a previous round of cutbacks. In addition to the creation of The Royal Highland Fusiliers, The Seaforth Highlanders had amalgamated with Queen's Own Cameron Highlanders to form Queen's Own Highlanders in 1961, but joining forces with another Lowland regiment, most likely The King's Own Scottish Borderers, was not an option which the regiment was willing to take. When the news arrived in 1967, shortly after the battalion had returned from its successful tour in Aden, soundings were taken within the battalion and the regimental family and the decision was taken to disband. On 18 July 1967 Healey announced the cuts, which included the following statement: 'Lowland Brigade. The brigade will reduce by one battalion which is to be 1st Cameronians (Scottish Rifles). The

Council of Colonels did not recommend an amalgamation with any other regiment.' A similar decision was taken by The York and Lancaster Regiment (65th and 84th), which traced its history back to 1756. These were the first disbandments since 1922, when the army's five southern Irish regiments were removed from the Army List as a result of Irish independence.

The reasons for the decision to disband were reasonably transparent. Speaking in the House of Lords on 25 July 1967, when the Defence White Paper was being debated, Lord Thurlow, a former Seaforth Highlander, said that The Cameronians was a regiment with a unique background and that 'no amalgamation is possible'. It is also possible that the decision was informed by memories of the Cardwell/Childers reforms and the subsequent rivalries between the 1st and 2nd battalions. Amongst retired members of the regiment there were hopes of a last-minute reprieve on account of the regiment's record of service. The Cameronians had a superb history and had performed well on its recent tour in Aden; it also had many well-connected supporters including four generals, three lieutenant-generals and six major-generals, a unique number in any regiment, as well as a good deal of private and public backing within Scotland. That was what happened a year later when The Argyll and Sutherland Highlanders, the junior Highland regiment, escaped a similar fate following a demand for further cutbacks in the infantry. Thanks to a high-profile and well-organised 'Save the Argylls' campaign, the regiment survived at company strength and was quietly returned to the Army List in 1972. By then a crisis had developed in Northern Ireland which required the army to intervene in answer to the request made by the government of Northern Ireland in August 1969 for the provision of troops to assist the civil power in restoring order following outbreaks of sectarian violence in Belfast and Londonderry.

However, in the case of The Cameronians a reprieve was never on the cards, and with a quiet and dignified stoicism which impressed everyone inside and outside the army The Cameronians accepted the fate that had been meted out. The battalion's commanding officer, Lieutenant-Colonel Leslie Dow, made a spirited appeal for a final overseas tour and for disbandment to be postponed until 1970 in order to maintain morale but this was rejected. With no other options open to it, the regiment decided to disband the following year, 1968, at the same place that it had been raised 279 years earlier. Dow gauged correctly that any hesitation or postponement would harm the regiment and that a long period of wind-down in a home posting would not help those younger soldiers who still had their careers in front of them. Preparations were put in hand to transfer serving officers and men to other formations throughout the army, the majority selecting the regiments of the Scottish Division. Plans were also laid for the final disbandment parade, which would be held at Douglas in Lanarkshire on 14 May 1968. It was preceded by a number of farewell parades in the regimental area and by a final Beating of Retreat at Edinburgh Castle.

On the day itself the 250 men taking part in the parade left Redford Barracks in Edinburgh and were taken to Douglas, where they formed up in three companies behind the pipes and drums. There were many others there to see them march into history – the regimental colonel, Lieutenant-General Sir George Collingwood, the Duke of Hamilton, the GOC Scotland Lieutenant-General Sir Derek Lang – but the day belonged to the regiment, not just to the serving soldiers but also to the 'old and bold' who made good the saying, 'once a Cameronian, aye a Cameronian'. For a regiment steeped in the Covenanting tradition it was right and proper that the ceremony should culminate in a conventicle, with the communion table standing on a spur of ground close to Castle Dangerous, the former Douglas stronghold. Piquets were then posted to protect the conventicle – a necessary precaution in the covenanting days and a tradition preserved by the regiment. The service was led by Dr Donald MacDonald, who received the words to begin from the piquet officer: 'Reverend Sir, the piquets are posted, there is no enemy in sight, the service may proceed.' MacDonald's moving testament matched the occasion (see Chapter One) and there were also messages from HRH Queen Elizabeth II, from the Colonel-in-Chief King Gustav VI of Sweden and from General Collingwood, who spoke of the pride all Cameronians could feel in the regiment's long and proud history. As the service drew to a close Colonel Dow approached General Lang, saluted, and asked permission to disband: 'We have to go now, sir, it is time for us to go.' The regimental flag was lowered and marched to the communion table. The bugles sounded, Pipe-Major Gillies played the moving lament 'The Flowers of the Forest', and after three centuries of service to the country The Cameronians (Scottish Rifles) was no more. It was as MacDonald had told them:

> Today, you cease to be a regular arm of Her Majesty's forces.
> It has never been the habit of Cameronians to whimper
> and we shall not whimper now, for, thank God, we can fill
> this doleful moment with gratitude and pride.

Forty years after The Cameronians (Scottish Rifles) disbanded, the regimental trustees decided to mark the anniversary by holding a final gathering and conventicle at Douglas on Sunday, 11 May 2008. By the cairn which marks the spot where the Earl of Angus raised his regiment, former soldiers paraded and remembered the old 26th and 90th. By then even deeper changes had affected the Scottish regimental system. In 1994 a further round of defence cuts in the aftermath of the end of the Cold War and the collapse of communism in eastern Europe had led to the amalgamation of Queen's Own Highlanders with The Gordon Highlanders to form The Highlanders, but this was as nothing compared with what took place ten years later. This time the change was even more radical and far-reaching, as it involved a comprehensive restructuring of the infantry. Under these changes the size of the infantry was reduced from 40 to 36 battalions and that meant the end of the remaining 19 single-battalion regiments. In their place 16 regiments maintained the traditions of the British infantry – five foot guards, nine new large infantry regiments with several Regular and Territorial battalions, one Irish regiment and the Parachute Regiment. In Scotland the new formation was called The Royal Regiment of Scotland, consisting of five Regular battalions and two Territorial battalions. Its formation day was 28 March 2006. Senior officers insisted that the 'golden thread' linking the new regiment to the past would be maintained, and although by then The Cameronians (Scottish Rifles) was long gone, there were vestiges of its presence. The regiment's 1st battalion, formed by an amalgamation of The Royal Scots with The King's Own Scottish Borderers, wears the black hackle of The Cameronians and the 52nd Lowland 6th battalion still retains The Cameronians in its regimental lineage. (The final Cameronian element, D Company was rebadged as King's Own Scottish Borderers in 1997.) It is not much, but as John Baynes put it in his preface to his fine study of the 2nd Scottish Rifles at Neuve Chapelle, 'thank God, it is something!'

Appendix

REGIMENTAL FAMILY TREE
1st battalion (26th)

1689: The Cameronian Regiment

1751: The 26th Regiment of Foot (The Cameronians)

1803: 2nd battalion raised

1814: 2nd battalion disbanded

1881: 1st battalion The Cameronians (Scottish Rifles)

1946: 1st battalion placed in suspended animation

2nd battalion (90th)

1794: 90th Regiment of Foot, Perthshire Volunteers; 2nd battalion raised

1795: 2nd battalion transferred to Royal Marines

1804: new 2nd battalion raised

THE CAMERONIANS

1815: 90th Perthshire Light Infantry

1817: new 2nd battalion disbanded

1881: 2nd battalion The Cameronians (Scottish Rifles)

1946: renumbered 1st battalion

1st battalion (26th/90th)

1968: regiment disbanded

REGIMENTAL BADGE

The regimental badge is a Mullet (star) of the coat of arms of the Douglas family, upon a stringed bugle horn, within two sprays of thistles.

REGIMENTAL TARTANS

The regiment did not wear tartan until 1881 and the introduction of territorial allegiances under the Cardwell/Childers reforms. Like the other Lowland regiments The Cameronians (Scottish Rifles) used the Government or Black Watch tartan when wearing trews. Ten years later, in 1891, it was authorised to wear the Douglas tartan in recognition of its links to the family. As a rifle regiment officers and men wore tunics of traditional rifle green. The pipers wore kilts of Douglas tartan.

REGIMENTAL PIPE MUSIC

Pipers were not officially recognised by the army until 1854, when all Highland regiments were allowed a pipe-major and five pipers. Before that most Highland regiments employed pipers as a regimental expense and these were distributed throughout the regiment disguised on the muster roll as 'drummers'. Pipers were present in the 26th and the 90th before 1881 when both battalions had pipes and drums in addition to the military band. The pipers in the 2nd battalion adopted grey sporrans with three black tassels to differentiate them from the 1st battalion pipers, who wore a black sporran with two white tassels. As a rifle regiment The Cameronians marched at 140 paces per minute and the instrument of command and routine was the bugle.

The regimental music is regularised as follows:

Regimental Band: Within a Mile of Edinburgh Toun

March Past in Quick Time, 1st Battalion: Kenmuir's on an' Awa

March Past in Quick Time, 2nd Battalion: The Gathering of the Grahams

BATTLE HONOURS

As a rifle regiment, The Cameronians carried no colours after the amalgamation of 1881. Instead the battle honours were carried on its 'appointments' (usually the drums). In common with all line-infantry regiments, the 26th carried two colours, the King's or Queen's, which was the Union flag, and the Regimental Colour (originally First and Second Colour), which was buff.

During the Napoleonic wars battle honours were added to the colours but these were given sparingly or even randomly. In 1882 the system of battle honours was revised by a War Office committee under the chairmanship of General Sir Archibald Alison. It laid down guidelines whereby only victories would be included and the majority of the regiment had to be present. Additional refinements were made in 1907 and 1909 and their recommendations form the basis of the regiment's pre-1914 battle honours.

Pre-1914 (26th and 90th)

Blenheim	Corunna	Lucknow
Ramillies	Martinique 1809	Abyssinia
Oudenarde	Guadeloupe 1810	South Africa 1877, '78, '7'
Malplaquet	South Africa 1846–47	Relief of Ladysmith
Mandora	Sevastopol	South Africa 1899–1902

After the First World War there were further refinements to take cognisance of the size and complexity of the conflict. It was agreed that each regiment could carry ten major honours on their King's Colour but supporting operations would also receive battle honours which would not be displayed. Those in bold type are the main battle honours

The First World War (27 battalions)

Mons	Arleux	Canal du Nord
Le Cateau	**Ypres 1917, '18**	St Quentin Canal
Retreat from Mons	Pilckem	Cambrai 1918
Marne 1914–18	Langemarck 1917	Courtrai
Aisne 1914	Menin Road	Selle
La Bassée 1914	Polygon Wood	Sambre
Armentières 1914	Passchendaele	France and Flanders
Neuve Chapelle	St Quentin	1914–18
Aubers	Roslères	Doiran 1917, '18
Loos	Avre	**Macedonia 1915–18**
Somme 1916–18	Lys	**Gallipoli 1915–16**
Albert 1916	Hazebrouck	Rumani
Bazentin	Bailleul	Egypt 1916–17

Pozières	Kemmel	**Gaza**
Flers–Courcelette	Scherpenberg	El Mughar
Le Transloy	Soissonnais-Ourcq	Nebi Shamwil
Ancre Heights	Drocourt-Quéant	Jaffa
Arras 1917–18	**Hindenburg Line**	**Palestine 1917–18**
Scarpe 1917–18	Epéhy	

In 1956 it was agreed to treat the Second World War in the same
way as the previous conflict.

The Second World War (seven battalions)

Ypres–Comines Canal	Asten	Simeto Bridgehead
Odon	Roer	**Sicily 1943**
Cheux	**Rhineland**	Garigliano Crossing
Caen	Reichswald	Anzio
Mont Pincon	Moyland	Advance to Tiber
Estry	**Rhine**	**Italy 1943–44**
Nederrijn	Dreierwalde	Pogu 1942
Best	Bremen	Paungde
Scheldt	Artlenberg	Yenagyaung 1942
South Beveland	**North-west Europe 1940, 1944–45**	**Chindits 1944**
Walcheren Causeway	Landing in Sicily	**Burma 1942, '44**

ALLIED AND AFFILIATED REGIMENTS

7th Duke of Edinburgh's Own Gurkha Rifles

Canada

The Perth Regiment

Australia

26th Battalion The Logan and Albert Regiment

New Zealand

The Otago and Southland Regiment

Ghana

2nd Battalion Ghana Regiment of Infantry

South Africa

The Witwatersrand Rifles

WINNERS OF THE VICTORIA CROSS

Private John Alexander, 90th Perthshire Light Infantry, Crimea, 1855

Born in Mullingar in County Westmeath, Ireland, Alexander was awarded the Victoria Cross for two separate displays of courage during the siege of Sevastopol in 1855. In the first incident he brought in several wounded men under heavy fire and in the second he rescued an officer in the Scots Fusilier Guards, again under heavy fire. Unfortunately Alexander never received his medal as he was killed two years later during the relief of Lucknow in the Indian Mutiny.

Sergeant Andrew Moynihan, 90th Perthshire Light Infantry, Crimea, 1855

During the attack on the Redan position Moynihan's storming party succeeded in killing a number of Russians. In the course of the action he rescued a wounded officer under fire and was himself wounded. Later in the campaign he was commissioned in the 8th Foot (later King's Liverpool Regiment) and reached the rank of captain. A native of Wakefield, Yorkshire, he died in Malta in 1867. His son, Major-General Berkeley Moynihan, helped to set up the medical services in the British Expeditionary Force in 1914.

Surgeon Anthony Home, 90th Perthshire Light Infantry, Indian Mutiny, 1857

Anthony Dickson Home, a graduate of the University of St Andrews, was in charge of the wounded men in the residency at Lucknow. When his escort was reduced in size through casualties, Home continued treating the men under fire and led the small party to a small shed where they continued a spirited resistance for 22 hours before being rescued. Later, he took part in the Ashanti War of 1874 and died 40 years later in the rank of Surgeon-General, a few days after the outbreak of the First World War.

Assistant-Surgeon William Bradshaw, 90th Perthshire Light Infantry, Indian Mutiny, 1857

Awarded to Bradshaw in the same action at Lucknow. As Home's assistant he remained with the wounded and organised their retreat to safety after the dhooly-bearers had retired. A native of Thurles in County Tipperary, he died there in 1861 and is buried in St Mary's Churchyard.

Major John Guise, 90th Perthshire Light Infantry, Indian Mutiny, 1857

Born in Gloucestershire in 1826, Guise was commissioned into the regiment in 1843 and at the time had just achieved his majority. He was awarded the Victoria Cross during the attack on the Sikandarbagh where he helped to rescue wounded men under heavy fire. He was elected to receive the award by his fellow officers. Later he commanded the 90th and died in 1895 in the rank of Lieutenant-General. He was buried in Gorey, County Wexford.

Sergeant Samuel Hill, 90th Perthshire Light Infantry, Indian Mutiny, 1857

One of the many Irish men who have served in Scottish regiments, Hill enlisted in the 67th Foot before transferring to the 90th. He was involved in the same incident as Major Guise and was awarded the Victoria Cross for saving the life of a wounded officer. He was elected for the award by the regiment. He died in Meerut, India, in 1863.

Private Patrick Graham, 90th Perthshire Light Infantry, Indian Mutiny, 1857

In the final stages of the fighting to regain the residency at Lucknow Graham brought in a wounded soldier while under heavy fire. He was elected for the award by his fellow soldiers. A native of Dublin, he died in the city in 1875.

Lieutenant William Rennie, 90th Perthshire Light Infantry, Indian Mutiny, 1857

Having been commissioned from the ranks in 1854, Rennie charged the enemy's guns at Lucknow and prevented them from being dragged to safety in advance of the British attack. In another incident he again attacked the guns in spite of coming under heavy grape fire. Later he was promoted lieutenant-colonel and died in his native Elgin in 1896.

Lieutenant William Lysons, 90th Perthshire Light Infantry, Zulu War, 1879

The son of a distinguished general, Lysons was commissioned into the 90th in 1878 and was awarded the Victoria Cross for dislodging the enemy from their position on Inhlobane Mountain and driving them away. An accompanying officer of the Coldstream Guards was killed in the same incident. Lysons was later promoted colonel and died in London in 1907.

Private Edmund Fowler, 90th Perthshire Light Infantry, Zulu War, 1879

Awarded the Victoria Cross for his courage during the action involving Lieutenant Lysons on Inhlobane Mountain. It took three years for both awards to be gazetted, by which time the regiment had become 2nd Cameronians (Scottish Rifles). Born in Waterford, Fowler died in Colchester in March 1926.

Private Henry May, 1st Cameronians, First World War, 1914

In two separate incidents near La Bouteillerie in northern France May exposed himself to severe enemy fire in an attempt to rescue wounded men. One of them, Lieutenant Douglas Graham, went on to become a major-general and a colonel of the regiment. May recovered from his wounds and was later commissioned in the Army Service Corps. A native of Glasgow, he died there in July 1941.

Lance-Corporal John Erskine, 5th Cameronians, First World War, 1916

The only Cameronian soldier from a Territorial battalion to be awarded the Victoria Cross, John Erskine was a teacher's son from

Dunfermline and had been apprenticed as a draper before joining up. At Givenchy on 22 June 1916 he rescued an officer under heavy fire and helped to bring him in by using his own body as a shield. He was killed at Arras a year later.

Private James Towers, 2nd Cameronians, First World War, 1918

A month before the Armistice, during the Second Battle of Le Cateau, Towers volunteered to act as a runner even though five others had already been killed. Despite coming under heavy fire he managed to ensure that the vital message was delivered. He was born in Preston, Lancashire, in 1897 and died there 80 years later.

Bibliography

Unless otherwise stated, extracts from soldiers' letters and diaries are in the possession of the regiment or are housed in the Imperial War Museum or the National Army Museum, London. Quotations from battalion and brigade War Diaries or other official papers are housed in the National Archives, Kew. The regimental magazine is *The Covenanter*.

BOOKS ABOUT THE CAMERONIANS

Barclay, Brigadier C. N., *The History of The Cameronians (Scottish Rifles)*, vol. III, 1933–1946, Sifton Praed, London, 1949

Baynes, John, *Morale: A Study of Men and Courage, The Second Scottish Rifles at the Battle of Neuve Chapelle*, Cassell, London, 1967; *The History of The Cameronians (Scottish Rifles)*, vol. IV, Cassell, London, 1971

Baynes, John and Maclean, Hugh, eds, *A Tale of Two Captains*, The Pentland Press, Edinburgh, 1990

Carter, Thomas, ed., *The Historical Records of the Twenty-Sixth or Cameronian Regiment*, Byfield Stanford and Co., London, 1867

Cockburn, Robert, *Fierce is the Foray and Far is the Cry*, Trustees of The Cameronians (Scottish Rifles), 2004

Courtenay, A. H., *With the 4th Battalion The Cameronians (Scottish Rifles) in South Africa 1900–1901*, privately published, 1905

Crichton, Andrew, *The Life and Diary of Lieutenant-Colonel J. Blackader of the Cameronian Regiment*, H. S. Baynes, Edinburgh, 1824

Darling, Lieutenant-Colonel John Stormonth, *Memoir*, Standard Press, Kilmarnock, 1923

Delavoye, A. M., *Records of the 90th Regiment (Perthshire Light Infantry) 1795–1880*, Richardson & Co., London, 1880

Findlay, Colonel J. M., *With the 8th Scottish Rifles 1914–1919*, Blackie, Glasgow and London, 1926

Grant, Philip R., *The Generals*, Trustees of The Cameronians (Scottish Rifles), 2005; *The Bravest of the Brave*, Trustees of The Cameronians (Scottish Rifles), 2007; *The Formation of The Cameronians (Scottish Rifles) 26th and 90th*, Trustees of The Cameronians (Scottish Rifles), 2007

Jack, Brigadier-General J.L., *General Jack's Diary*, John Terraine, ed., Eyre & Spottiswoode, London, 1964

Johnston, S. H. F., *The History of The Cameronians (Scottish Rifles)*, vol. I, 1689–1910, Gale & Polden, Aldershot, 1957

Lawson, John Burnett, *Cameronian Officer*, John Smith, Glasgow, 1921

Reid, Douglas Arthur, *Memories of the Crimean War January, 1855 to June 1856*, St Catherine Press, London, 1911

Reith, Lord, *Wearing Spurs*, Hutchinson, London, 1966

Story, Colonel H. H., *The History of the Cameronians*, vol II., The Regiment, Hamilton, 1961

White, Rev. John, *With The Cameronians (Scottish Rifles) in France: Leaves from a Chaplain's Diary*, privately published, 1917

Wylly, H. C., *A Short History of The Cameronians (Scottish Rifles)*, Gale & Polden, Aldershot, 1924

OTHER BOOKS CONSULTED

Ascoli, David, *A Companion to the British Army 1660–1983*, Harrap, London, 1983

Barnett, Correlli, *Britain and her Army 1509–1970*, Allen Lane, London, 1970; *The Lost Victory: British Dreams, British Realities 1945–1950*, Macmillan, London, 1995

Baynes, John, *The Forgotten Victor: General Sir Richard O'Connor*, Brassey's, London, 1989

Baynes, John, with Laffin, John, *Soldiers of Scotland*, Brassey's, London, 1988

Brereton, J. M., *The British Army: A Social History of the British Army from 1661 to the Present Day*, The Bodley Head, London, 1986

Chandler, David, and Beckett, Ian, eds, *The Oxford Illustrated History of the British Army*, Oxford University Press, Oxford, 1994

Cockburn, Lord, *Journal*, Edmonston and Douglas, Edinburgh, 1875

David, Saul, *The Indian Mutiny 1857*, Viking, London, 2002

Doyle, Arthur Conan, *The Great Boer War*, Smith Elder, London, 1900

Ewing, John, *History of the 9th (Scottish) Division 1914–1919*, John Murray, London, 1921

Fortescue, Sir John, *A History of the British Army*, 13 vols, Macmillan, London, 1899–1930

Henderson, Diana M., *The Scottish Regiments*, Collins, Glasgow, 1996

Hislop, Alexander, ed., *The Book of Scottish Anecdote, Humorous, Social, Legendary and Historical*, Thomas D. Morrison, Glasgow, 1880

Holmes, Richard, ed., *The Oxford Companion to Military History*, Oxford University Press, Oxford, 2001

Jackson, Bill and Bramall, Dwin, *The Chiefs: The Story of the United Kingdom Chiefs of Staff*, Brassey's, London, 1992

Keegan, John, *Six Armies in Normandy*, Jonathan Cape, London, 1982

Kinglake, A. W., *The Invasion of the Crimea*, 8 vols, William Blackwood, Edinburgh and London, 1863–87

Martin, Lieutenant-General H. G., *The Fifteenth Scottish Division 1939–1945*, William Blackwood, Edinburgh and London, 1948

Massey, W. T., *How Jerusalem was Won, Being the Record of Allenby's Campaign in Palestine*, Constable, London, 1919

Masters, John, *The Road Past Mandalay*, Michael Joseph, London, 1961

Mileham, P. J. R., *Scottish Regiments*, Spellmount, Tunbridge Wells, 1988

Neillands, Robin, *A Fighting Retreat: The British Empire 1947–1997*, Hodder & Stoughton, London, 1996

Roberts, Lord, *Forty-One Years in India*, 2 vols, Richard Bentley, London, 1897

Royle, Trevor, *The Best Years of Their Lives: The National Service Experience 1945–1963*, Michael Joseph, London, 1986; *Orde Wingate: Irregular Soldier*, Weidenfeld and Nicolson, 1995; *Crimea: The Great Crimean War 1854–1856*, Little Brown, London, 1999

Stewart of Garth, David, *Sketches of the Character, Manners and present State of the Highlanders of Scotland, with details of the Military Service of the Highland Regiments*, 2 vols, Constable, Edinburgh, 1822

Stewart, J., and Buchan, John, *The 15th (Scottish) Division 1914–1919*, William Blackwood, Edinburgh and London, 1926

Strawson, John, *Gentlemen in Khaki: The British Army 1890–1990*, Hutchinson, London, 1989; *Beggars in Red: The British Army 1789–1889*, Hutchinson, London, 1991

Talbot, F. E.G., *The 14th King George's Own Sikhs 1846–1933*, Royal United Services Institute, London, 1937

BIBLIOGRAPHY

Wakefield, Alan, and Moody, Simon, *Under the Devil's Eye: Britain's Forgotten Army at Salonika 1915–1918*, Sutton Publishing, Stroud, 2004

Wolseley, Field Marshal Viscount, *The Story of a Soldier's Life*, 2 vols, Constable, London, 1903

Wood, Sir Evelyn, *From Midshipman to Field Marshal*, 2 vols, Methuen, London, 1906

Wood, Stephen, *The Scottish Soldier*, Archive Publications, Manchester, 1987

WEBSITES

http://www.cameronians.org/ Cameronian Museum

http://www.grandfathersgreatwar.com/ Diary of Captain Alexander Stewart

http://www.geocities.com/nicolgrahame/letters.htm Letters of Lieutenant Nicol Grahame

http://www.aboutms.co.uk/walk/walk.htm A Soldier's Tears by Jack Rafferty. 7th Battalion The Cameronians Multiple Sclerosis Research Initiative

Index

INDEX

INDEX

INDEX

INDEX